LOST WASHINGTON, D.C.

Author credits
Thanks to librarian Jerry McCoy of the Peabody Room, Georgetown Library, and the Washingtoniana Division of the Martin L. King, Jr. Memorial Library, along with the Prints and Photographs Division of the Library of Congress. My editors Frank Hopkinson and David Salmo of Anova Books, and my partner Gregory J. Alexander for his editorial leadership and patience.

Picture credits
All images are courtesy of the Library of Congress, except for the following:
Anova Image Library: 55, 77, 82 (left), 102 (top), 107 (right), 111 (left).
Corbis: 11, 38 (left and center), 58 (left), 64, 76, 89 (left), 96, 97 (left), 104 (left), 105, 114, 136–137, 140 (top left).
Getty: 51, 90, 92 (left), 93, 122 (left), 123, 132.
Paul Kelsey Williams: 30, 39, 49 (left), 50 (top), 52–53, 56, 59, 66–69, 72–73, 75 (right), 78–79, 81 (right), 84–85, 95 (top), 97 (top right), 98 (left), 99, 102 (bottom), 108, 110, 111 (right), 112–113, 116–117, 124–125, 130–131, 135 (bottom), 140 (top right).

Endpapers
Front: View of Washington, circa 1850.
Back: Bird's-Eye View of Washington from the Potomac—Looking North, circa 1880.

First published in the United Kingdom in 2012 by
PAVILION BOOKS
10 Southcombe Street, London W14 0RA
An imprint of Anova Books Company Ltd

© Anova Books, 2012

Project managers: Frank Hopkinson and David Salmo.

ISBN: 978-1-86205-993-1

A CIP catalogue record for this book is available from the British Library.

10 9 8 7 6 5 4 3 2 1

Repro by Rival Colour Ltd, UK
Printed by 1010 Printing International Ltd, China

www.anovabooks.com

LOST WASHINGTON, D.C.

Paul Kelsey Williams

PAVILION

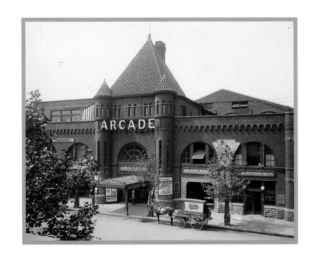

LOST IN THE...

FOREWORD

Okay, I'll blow the lid on a secret of Washington reporting: when journalists in the capital of the free world are hot on a story about some local character, and the reporter is trying to build a full and dramatic tale of a subject's rise to power or fall from grace, the savvy journo knows exactly whom to call—Paul Williams, the house historian.

One call, and suddenly your story is laced with exquisite and telling details about where your main character came from and how he grew up and who his family was and what shaped him. Williams knows all this—or can find out for you in a jiffy—because he is Washington's preeminent explorer of the city's built past. And that turns out to be not a dry terrain of architectural detail, but a rich, living history of the people and relationships that make a house a home. That's why so many Washingtonians turn to Paul Williams to discover who has lived in their house in the past, and how that house came to be where and what it is.

I first learned how and why Paul does what he does when I spent a couple of days trailing him around town while he delved into the history of the house my family had just bought. There was, I thought, nothing unusual about our house. But watching Paul as he moved from the National Archives, to the D.C. Archives, to the Recorder of Deeds office, and on through the other great and neglected repositories of the city's past, I saw a total pro in action: he knew where to find the original plans for the house, and how to parlay that information into a profile of the builder and developer of the property, and how to work through census and other demographic resources to tease out who had lived in the house.

He moved with the grace and efficiency of a hunter through libraries and databases, so that within a few days, he could write a real story of Washington, and now my house, which I'd thought of merely as a building I'd bought from someone who'd owned it for a decade or so, was connected to Thomas Jefferson and the founding of the Marine Band and the birth of Italian immigration to America and so on all the way up to a 1970s cult—phew!

The houses and buildings in this book have three things in common: they are lost, either to the march of progress or the short-sightedness of greed; they tell stories about what the capital city was and wanted to be; and they are found again, because Williams has treated them just as he does the houses that still stand today—as living and revealing artifacts of a city that symbolizes American history, yet too often lives only in the present.

From the Civil War encampments through which Walt Whitman walked as he contemplated the meaning of a nation's suffering, to the Rhodes Tavern, a landmark near the White House that everyone knew was an essential piece of history, the places of the past disappear, sometimes because they were only meant to be temporary and sometimes because some powerful person believes he has an idea superior to that of history.

But what emerges in the profiles that follow is not a preservationist's lament of the foolish or selfish decisions of those who raze our collective treasures, but a celebration of places that captured who we were, the buildings that reveal to us even now the passions that shaped Washington. Here is where those who came before us played (in a floating theater on the Potomac, at the Republic Theater, in an underground jazz club complete with stalactites and stalagmites) and prayed (in a magnificent church with the city's highest steeple, in a stadium where Senators taught daily lessons in humility) and of course practiced the hometown art of the possible, the craft of politics (in saloons and opera houses, grand hotels and sleazy hideaways). The buildings may be gone, but the legends they spawned were just waiting to be excavated, which is exactly what Williams has done here.

A hundred years from now, when the next Williams is on the hunt for the stories to fill the next volume of *Lost Washington, D.C.*, he will need a wholly different toolbox, searching for traces of the electronic trail we left behind as we lived in today's houses, clubs, bars, eateries and offices. But when it comes time to make sense of the data that future prospector collects, he will no doubt turn to this book to learn how his mountain of facts translates into the story of those who called this home.

Marc Fisher
The Washington Post

INTRODUCTION

Washington, D.C. witnessed the loss of architectural structures and the built environment soon after it was designated the nation's capital in 1801. Early country estates and farms were demolished to make way for a grand redesign of the city. By 1814, most of the city's spectacular new public buildings, including the White House, and military institutions such as the Navy Yard, were either burned by the invading British Army during the War of 1812, or set afire by retreating American troops lest they fell into the hands of the enemy.

Washington, D.C. remained a relatively small city up until the Civil War, when tens of thousands of military units and supporting troops settled into and onto just about any building or park that could be commandeered. Following the war's end in 1865, the impressive rings of forts, military hospitals, training facilities and storage depots were mostly dismantled and razed. The massive influx into Washington of freed blacks and others devastated by the war created the first major housing crisis. The city lost many of its wood-frame houses and low lying buildings to make way for larger apartment buildings, hotels, and rooming houses.

As the city grew, the downtown core changed from its rows of traditional Federal-styled townhouses, mostly razed by 1900, to give way to blocks entirely occupied by a single hotel or office building. The federal government grew as well, and massive buildings such as the Library of Congress and the Supreme Court caused the loss of thousands of houses and other architectural remnants of the city's early history.

By the 1960s, when the automobile was king, expressways like the Whitehurst Freeway covered what had been the port of Georgetown, while other structures that were never actually built caused widespread demolition during their early planning stages. Perhaps no city in the United States witnessed the systematic relocation of an entire neighborhood as large as Southwest D.C., with its tens of thousands of houses razed to make way for a new city of high-rise apartment buildings.

Anyone interested in Washington's lost buildings has no doubt perused James M. Goode's *Capital Losses*. Goode's book offers a wide array of buildings, houses, and structures that are no longer extant and it is considered the bible of what the city has tragically lost to fire, planning, expansion, and changes in technology over time. Some of the resources found here are also covered in Goode's book due to their significance. However, *Lost Washington* brings the story up to date, including many buildings that have been lost since the 1970s. This book also delves behind the city's architectural history to reveal fascinating details of the occupants and events that marked Washington's lost buildings.

A diverse range of houses, buildings, and structures once found along the streets in Washington, D.C. are included here. They range from a popular nightclub on U Street designed to resemble a cave, to the original Washington airport that was once located on what is now the site of the Pentagon. The reasons for the loss can be as natural as a fire, or as impersonal as a need for a staging area for the Metro system.

Other inclusions are meant to surprise and delight at what once was, or offer a peek into lifestyles and living rooms that will never be repeated. Some shed light on local mysteries, such as why one can find a lock keeper's cottage on Constitution Avenue and 17th Street, located far from any water today. Some resources, such as the numerous Civil War encampments were disbanded as early as 1865 while others were razed and lost as recently as 1995, when the last remnants of the Children's Hospital were removed, ending a 110-year legacy of treating the city's youngest residents. The buildings and structures included in *Lost Washington, D.C.* range from a small but significant horse watering trough to the entire Southwest neighborhood, systematically and nearly wholly razed in the 1960s.

While the physical structures might be gone, the outstanding resources in various Washington research centers such as the Prints and Photographs Division of the Library of Congress, the Washingtoniana Room at Martin Luther King Jr., Memorial Library, and the Historical Society of Washington hold clues and photographs to discover, document, and preserve the city's lost history. It is my hope that this book might also be used one day as a history lesson to remind and highlight what Washington's residents and tourists alike have so carelessly lost in the past, and to help educate future generations not to repeat the cycle.

Paul Kelsey Williams

Civil War Encampments DISBANDED 1865

According to an official Army report, at the close of the Civil War in 1865, the city of Washington boasted 68 enclosed forts that held a total of 807 mounted cannons. The report included well-known fortifications such as Fort Lincoln, Fort Stevens, and Fort Totten, some of which remain to this day. Supporting these forts and providing housing and medical treatment, however, were dozens and dozens of temporary encampments and barracks that were located all across the city on virtually every piece of open land.

These encampments ranged from small tent cities to temporary wooden barracks and large-scale hospital complexes. While the area north of the downtown part of the city was mainly agricultural and orchard fields or woods, following the first few shots of the Civil War in 1861, the Union chose this area for some of the military's vast encampments. It includes areas in today's neighborhoods of Foggy Bottom, Greater U Street, Columbia Heights, and Shaw, among others. Even the center of well landscaped and developed circles such as Iowa Circle (Logan today) held an encampment, in this case allegedly containing a hangman's gallows to execute military deserters.

The encampments enabled the city to become a staging area for the Manassas Campaign, organized after the staggering defeat to the Confederacy at the First Battle of Bull Run by Brigadier General Irvin McDowell on July 21, 1861.

Larger encampments included Campbell Hospital at Sixth Street and Florida Avenue, NW, Wisewell Barracks at Seventh and P Streets, NW, Camp Barker at 13th and R Streets, NW, and Camp Brightwood at Georgia Avenue and Madison Street, NW. The camps offered a haven for freedmen fleeing from the South, with many choosing to stay after the war to establish permanent residency in the neighborhoods.

It was at Camp Brightwood where men used signal flags to communicate with nearby Fort DeRussy and the distant Capitol. It served as a transfer point for the wounded during the Battle of Fort Stevens on July 11 and 12, 1864, the only Civil War battle fought in the District of Columbia.

Many Washington families were conflicted with the virtual occupation, with estate owners having lost their crops and grazing lands. Others had two sons in the early conflict, one fighting for the North, and one for the South. There was apathy and Southern sympathy. Others like Julia Ward Howe, upon hearing a Union regiment singing "John Brown's Body" as the soldiers marched beneath her open window, wrote the patriotic "Battle Hymn of the Republic" to the same tune.

To illustrate the population surge during the war, the census reported just over 75,000 city residents in 1860. Ten years later, that number had blossomed to 132,000. The encampments often housed warehouses, ammunition depots, factories, sick wards, and thousands of military and civilians living in barracks or tents.

The extent of the large number of encampments by 1862 taking up all available land resulted in the Union army housing thousands of injured soldiers in commandeered hotels, schools, colleges, large estates, and churches.

Following the close of the Civil War in 1865, the encampments were slowly disbanded, with the wood beams and siding reused on small houses that cropped up in surrounding lands. Many areas returned to their agricultural basis until purchased and redeveloped by real estate speculators in the late 1870s to 1890s.

RIGHT *The Second Rhode Island Infantry Regiment was photographed in 1861 at Camp Jameson, part of the defenses surrounding Washington, D.C. during the Civil War.*

EMANCIPATION PROCLAMATION

Slavery was abolished in Washington, D.C. on April 16, 1862—a full eight months before Abraham Lincoln issued the Emancipation Proclamation that eventually led to the freeing of those enslaved throughout the country. Slave owners in the city—and there were plenty of them—were paid for their loss according to Lincoln's Compensated Emancipation Act. With surrounding States still imposing slavery, Washington became a popular place for freed slaves to congregate, and many were employed in the construction of the ring of fortresses that eventually surrounded the city. The Emancipation Memorial (also known as the Freedman's Memorial or the Emancipation Group) was erected in Lincoln Park on Capitol Hill in 1876. It was designed and sculpted by Thomas Ball, and paid for by African Americans. Frederick Douglass spoke at the dedication service attended by then President Ulysses S. Grant.

The Original Long Bridge REPLACED 1865

With the selection of Washington, D.C. as the Nation's Capital in 1800, there was no easy way to reach the southwestern portion of the city, which lay across the Potomac River, except by ferryboat. Investors seized an opportunity to construct a toll bridge, and the Washington Bridge Company was created by an Act of Congress on February 8, 1808 to construct the "Long Bridge" at the foot of 14th Street. President Thomas Jefferson signed the authorization into law.

The bridge was designed as a timber pile structure with two draw spans to connect the western end of Maryland Avenue at the foot of 14th Street, SW with the Virginia shore. The opening day was May 20, 1809. However, the northern portion of the bridge was burned by British troops who had invaded the city unopposed in August of 1814 and by 1816 the bridge had been completely rebuilt.

The low bridge was a constant source of grief for its owners, due to the number of times floods and an ice freshet would carry away sections of the traverse. The bridge had been badly damaged in 1831 by an ice freshet, and ferry service had once again been created to carry the traffic. Another freshet closed the bridge from 1840 to 1843.

With the expansion of the railroads in and out of Washington, plans were made to install tracks across the bridge, but it was determined to be too unsteady for the heavy locomotives. Tracks were built leading up to the bridge, but an omnibus was used to carry lightly loaded cars pulled by horse across the fragile span.

ABOVE *Union soldiers and artillery circa 1863 in front of a hotel along the railroad tracks that lead to the Long Bridge.*
OPPOSITE PAGE *Union troops stand guard in May of 1865 at the end of the Long Bridge, seen from the city.*
BELOW *Fort Richardson guarded the approach to the Long Bridge, the city's main link to Virginia.*

The bridge was again washed out by a flood in February 1857, but was reopened by the end of the year, as revenue service on the Alexandria and Washington Railway with connecting service over the bridge began December 21, 1857. With the outbreak of the Civil War, the bridge became an important military asset. Union troops occupied the bridge from May 24, 1861.

Rails were placed on the bridge, and the new railroad connection opened February 9, 1862, but due to weight restrictions, horse power had to be used over the bridge. A new, stronger bridge was built about 100 feet downriver, and opened on February 21, 1865. The new bridge carried only railroad traffic, with the old one for other traffic. On November 15, 1865, with the end of the war, the U.S. Military Railroad gave the old bridge to the U.S. Department of the Interior. The new bridge became part of the Washington, Alexandria and Georgetown Railroad, leased by the Baltimore and Ohio Rail Road. The original Long Bridge was disassembled following the Civil War.

Mason Island Ferry REPLACED BY BRIDGE CIRCA 1866

Analostan Island (now known as Theodore Roosevelt Island) is a 70-acre island situated on the Potomac across from Georgetown. It was purchased by Col. George Mason III in 1724 who bequeathed it to his son, the author of the landmark Virginia Bill of Rights. While ferries crossed the Potomac just north and south of the island as early as 1705, ferry service to Mason's Island (as it became known) wasn't licensed until 1748.

The large rock formation often pictured on the island in military photographs is known as Braddock's Rock, named after General Braddock who had assembled men of the 48th regiment there on April 12, 1755. Civilian ferry service increased in the 1790s, as the planning for the federal city required frequent trips across the river by Thomas Jefferson and George Washington. Several bridges were built as early as 1809 (see Long Bridge, page 13), but ferry service continued as a commercial enterprise.

Mason's estate and ferry were illustrated on Robert King's 1818 map of Washington.

Subsequent Mason family members inhabited the island until it was advertised for sale in 1834, and again in 1836. It was eventually purchased in 1850 by William A. Bradley, postmaster for the City of Washington. He built wharves and a dancing saloon in an attempt to attract tourists to his growing resort.

Union troops occupied the island at the beginning of the Civil War, guarding the ferry dock and ferry service. When the first two regiments of black volunteers were assembled in Washington, they were stationed at the island to protect them from harassment. The abandoned Mason house burned during the Civil War, and in 1865 a pontoon bridge linked the island to Georgetown. Following the war, Bradley again used the island for entertainment and enlarged the narrow causeway that led to the Virginia shore. The ferry service was discontinued just a few years later. The Washington Gas Light company bought the island in 1913 and it was sold in 1931 to the Roosevelt Memorial Association, who built the monument located on the site today.

FERRIES ACROSS THE POTOMAC

Many ferry services came and went on the Potomac, almost 100 in all throughout the history of the city of Washington, D.C. One had been chartered near Mason's Island in 1738 by Francis Awbrey, the owner of the popular Noland's Ferry farther upriver. The earliest ferry on the Potomac was licensed in 1705, located far to the south. They connected to postal routes on both sides of the river. Conrad's Ferry—known today as White's Ferry—is the only remaining ferry service on the Potomac. Located near Dickerson, Maryland, the ferry transports cars, trucks, pedestrians and bikers utilizing a cable system from Virginia and Maryland shorelines. It was established during the Civil War, but it had replaced Conrad's Ferry established on the site in 1817. Purchased by Confederate General Elijah V. White following the Civil War, he named it in honor of his former commander, General Jubal Anderson Early.

OPPOSITE PAGE *Guards checking a traveler's details while the Mason Island Ferry approaches.*

LEFT *The ferry boat carrying a team of horses and supplies.*

BELOW *The Aqueduct Bridge, connecting Washington, D.C. with Virginia, just south of Mason Island.*

Washington City Canal FILLED IN AND PAVED OVER 1871

In the early years of the United States, there was great interest in creating canals within cities emulating European counterparts. These were not for aesthetics, but for commerce. Pierre Charles L'Enfant included one in his design for the Capital City, but commissioners in 1792 deemed it too expensive to construct. A lottery held in 1796 to raise funds for its construction was unsuccessful.

In 1802, Congress granted a charter for the Washington Canal Company, and construction began in several portions of the planned route. The canal was to connect the Anacostia River (then known as the Eastern Branch), which was navigable into Maryland, with the Potomac, which was seen as a gateway to the West. It would later connect to the C&O Canal (see page 46).

Work at the beginning was slow and arduous. Congress created a new canal company in 1809 when the original had little to show for its effort, and funded it with $100,000. A groundbreaking ceremony with President James Madison took place on May 2, 1810 in southeast Washington. Construction commenced, but was suspended during the War of 1812.

The canal opened to much fanfare in November of 1815. It stretched from an entrance point near the Washington Navy Yard, proceeded north and west with several branches including James and Tiber creeks, and ran westerly exactly where Constitution Avenue exists today. It joined the Potomac River just south of the White House, long before the western half of the National Mall had been filled in.

The fanfare and hopes for the canal as a commercial success shortly faded, however, as silt and tidal nuances took their effect. The canal could only handle barges drawing a depth of three feet, eliminating most boat traffic. It was used moderately and suffered financial losses until the city purchased the canal company in 1831. Repairs fixed the problem of overflowing during high tide and empty portions during low tide.

In 1833, an extension of the C&O Canal was completed to incorporate the Washington Canal. Around 1835, a lock keeper's house was built at the eastern terminus of the C&O Canal, where it emptied into Tiber Creek and the Potomac River. The house still stands at the southwest corner of Constitution Avenue, and 17th Street, NW.

The canal was cleaned and dredged in 1849, but the city's promise to provide work and matching funds to Congressional budgets for the canal never materialized. In an era when most residents did not know how to swim, the canal provided a death trap to hundreds, especially young curious children or those wandering the city after a visit to a local saloon.

In the 1850s, Washington and other cities had begun to utilize railroads for most of the commerce transportation, and both the Washington and C&O canals were neglected. During the Civil War when the city's population boomed, the canal was used as a storm drain and open sewer. It was also a breeding ground for mosquitoes carrying malaria, and was such a health threat that it prompted the abandonment of the Van Ness mansion (see page 37).

Various proposals were introduced to either rehabilitate the city canal or fill it in. In 1871, the city's controversial head of Public Works, Alexander "Boss" Shepherd had the Tiber Creek portion of the canal covered over, which took years to complete. The new street that was constructed over this portion of the canal was initially designated as B Street, NW, but is known today as Constitution Avenue, NW.

The southern portion of the Washington City Canal remained open for years afterwards, but eventually was also paved over. A street constructed south of the Capitol over that section of the canal now connects Independence Avenue, SW, and E Street, SE. Formerly designated as Canal Street, the northernmost section of the street was later renamed Washington Avenue in commemoration of the state of Washington.

LEFT *This view of the Washington City Canal shows the United States Capitol under construction in 1860.*

RIGHT *The large width of the Washington City Canal can be seen in this western facing view, taken from the construction site of the Capitol dome. In the foreground is the octagonal greenhouse for the Botanic Garden. The Smithsonian's castle is in the background.*

The Port of Georgetown Shipping CEASED 1885

Few visitors to the neighborhood of Georgetown today would be able to imagine its waterfront park was once a thriving, industrial port. That's exactly what it was shortly after the founding of Georgetown in 1751, 50 years prior to the founding of the City of Washington that would eventually eclipse it. Georgetown would remain a separate municipality until 1871.

George Gordon constructed a tobacco inspection house on the river about 1745 where Georgetown exists today, at the fall line, the farthest point upstream on the Potomac River that ships could navigate. Tobacco had already been transported from adjoining farms to ships for several years, and it did not take long for the newly established port to grow with the addition of piers, wharves, warehouses, and other buildings used to transfer Maryland goods to ocean-going vessels for trade.

One of the most prominent tobacco export businesses was Forrest, Stoddert and Murdock, formed in 1783 by Uriah Forrest, Benjamin Stoddert, and John Murdock. Since Georgetown was founded during the reign of George II of Great Britain, some speculate that the town was named after him. The Maryland Legislature formally issued the town charter and incorporated the town in 1789. Robert Peter, who was among the first to establish a tobacco export business became Georgetown's first mayor in 1790.

In 1795, a custom house was established on Water Street, and General James M. Lingan served as the first collector of the port. The port thrived with the typical Colonial agricultural goods being shipped to Europe and with ships arriving offloading spices, building materials, and manufactured goods.

By the 1820s, the Potomac River had become silted up and was no longer navigable up to Georgetown for large ships. Construction of the Chesapeake & Ohio Canal began in 1828, to alleviate the silting problem, connecting Georgetown to Harper's Ferry, Virginia (now part of West Virginia). It provided a brief economic boost for Georgetown as its port was limited to transport boats and smaller schooners. Georgetown remained an important shipping center during the 1820s and 1830s, as tobacco and other goods were transferred between the canal and shipping on the Potomac River. Salt was imported from Europe, and sugar and molasses were imported from the West Indies. They were later superseded by coal and flour.

By the mid- to late 19th century, however, even the canal was susceptible to silt, and had to be continually dredged at a great cost. Combined with the then shallow Potomac also being compromised with low bridges, the fate of the Port of Georgetown as an industrial center was sealed. The increased capacity and network of the railroads in the decades following the Civil War led to the former port becoming more industrialized, with manufacturing replacing the shipping activities by 1885.

OPPOSITE PAGE *The vast Port of Georgetown is seen from Mason's Island in this Civil War-era photograph.*

BELOW *This image of the Port of Georgetown was taken by Andrew J. Russell between 1861 and 1865, showing the Long Bridge and Mason's Island in the background.*

Duddington Manor RAZED 1886

The intersection of Second and F Street, SE was once the location of a Federal-style mansion known as Duddington Manor. Its construction was begun in 1791 by Daniel Carroll of Duddington (1764–1849). The son of Charles Carroll of Carrollsburg, Daniel was the owner of what is today most of Capitol Hill, lands crucial to the planning of the Federal city. Charles Carroll had come to Maryland in 1680 after being appointed Attorney General of the colony by the Second Lord Baltimore. He was also one of the signatories of the Declaration of Independence.

Construction of Carroll's large manor house had begun nearby, where architect Pierre L'Enfant was insisting New Jersey Avenue be constructed. L'Enfant halted the construction of the manor house and destroyed its foundations. The ensuing fight was mediated by George Washington in Philadelphia and three local commissioners who convinced Carroll to build farther east. He was rewarded a $4,000 indemnity. In 1791, Carroll took ownership of the entire Square 736 as a site for the new house.

Duddington Manor was occupied by Daniel and Ann Rozier Carroll in 1793, although it was not completed until 1797. Carroll and other owners in the area assumed that the selection of the Potomac site for the new Federal city would make them more wealthy men than they already were. Recalling those times, Daniel Carroll wrote in 1837 that the results were other than expected:

I perfectly remember that the general opinion was that so great was the gift that the citizens never would be subject to taxation for the improvement of the streets having relinquished every alternate lot to the government. Instead some were so wild as to suppose ... that the government might pave the streets with ingots of gold or silver. After nearly a half century the result is now fully known; the unfortunate proprietors are generally brought to ruin and some with scarcely enough to buy daily food for their families.

Daniel Carroll and his father, who resided on a Georgian estate that is the site of Fort McNair today, set high prices on their land east of the Capitol building. Landowners to the west, however, undercut the prices, and substantial construction expanded in that direction for the next 100 years. Although substantially depleted, the Carrolls were far from destitute, remaining one of the largest landowners in Maryland. In 1800, Daniel Carroll had Carroll Row built as an investment. (See page 23.)

The odd footnote to the origin of Duddington revealed itself as the tale of two enemies. In the last years of his life and up until his death in 1825, Pierre L'Enfant was taken in by the Diggs family who owned the estate, renamed Green Hill. He was buried there until later being reinterred in Arlington Cemetery. The matron of the family, Mrs. Diggs, was none other than Eleanor Carroll, the daughter of Daniel Carroll, whose house had been razed by L'Enfant to accommodate his grand layout of Washington, D.C.

The Carroll family remained at the large estate for generations. It featured four acres of landscaped lawns, a smokehouse, and stable yard at what is today North Carolina Avenue and First Streets. It also had a creek that provided fresh water. The entire estate was enclosed at its borders with a brick wall. Received visitors included Presidents Washington, Adams, Jefferson, Madison, and Jackson.

Daniel Carroll died in 1849. His daughter continued to live there until 1886, when the house was sold for $60,000. It then suffered the same fate that cursed its original location; a street was cut through the property (Heckman Street), and plans were laid out to develop the two portions of the block into a townhouse development. The manor house was razed in 1886, when many of the present-day homes were built about its perimeter, including the entire 100 block of F Street in 1898 and a large house at the corner of First and F Streets in 1901.

The grand curving staircase of the manor house was saved and reinstalled in a house at 17th and Eye Streets, NW, until it, too, was razed in 1950.

ABOVE *Family members of Daniel Carroll gather on the front porch of Duddington Manor.*

RIGHT *The main staircase was removed in 1886 and reinstalled in a house at 17th and Eye Streets, NW, until it, too, was razed in 1950.*

OPPOSITE PAGE *A photograph of Duddington taken from the 1902 publication* Social Life in the Early Republic.

Carroll Row RAZED 1887

Residents of the five Federal styled townhouses located along present-day First Street, just north of A Street, would have had a fascinating view of the construction of the U.S. Capitol Building, which faced them. The row had begun being built in 1800 by Daniel Carroll of Duddington (see page 20).

The double-width building at the left (north) end was one of the city's first lodging establishments, known as the Long Hotel. It was here that the first inaugural ball was held on the second floor, celebrating the swearing in of President Madison in 1809. An invitee of the ball wrote that when it became so crowded and oppressive with heat, participants broke the glass on the sash windows, hopefully avoiding the elegant center Palladian window.

Just a few years later, following the burning of the city by the British on August 24, 1814, the row served as the headquarters for occupying General Robert Ross and Admiral Sir George Cockburn and their British forces. They utilized the house to the far right, owned by physician James Ewell, as a hospital for their injured soldiers. An addition built on the rear of his house in the 1830s was the home to the celebrated newspaper *United States Telegraph*, printed on site by editor Duff Green. He also printed most of the government records, books, and registers.

The large houses were well known as prestigious boardinghouses for various members of Congress, especially in the early years of the Republic when Washington was very short on housing. Future President John Quincy rented rooms, and Abraham Lincoln lived here from 1847 to 1849 while he served the 30th Congress.

During the Civil War, the row of houses was converted into the government's Carroll Prison, which housed hundreds of infamous political prisoners.

Like many of the early residential buildings surrounding the U.S. Capitol, Carroll Row was razed in 1887 to make way for federal offices and institutions. In this case, they were replaced by the elaborately designed main building of the Library of Congress. Architects John L. Smithmeyer and Paul J. Pelz had earlier won the competition for its design in 1873, and after several trips to Europe and numerous construction delays, were fired by Congress. The library was eventually constructed between 1890 and 1897.

ABOVE *Abraham Lincoln boarded in one of the Carroll Row houses he first served in the U.S. Congress. They were razed in 1887 for the main building of the Library of Congress.*

OPPOSITE PAGE *Carroll Row and Pennsylvania Avenue SE are seen in this image taken from the dome of the U.S. Capitol Building.*

Scott Hall, Soldiers' Home REMODELED 1868 AND 1890

Located on the U.S. Soldiers' Home campus, Scott Hall has housed veterans from every American War since the War of 1812. Construction began in 1851, but wasn't finished until 1857 due to a concern that the roof was faulty. The structure was significantly remodeled twice during its existence, obliterating the previous architectural style each time.

The original version was designed by second lieutenant Barton S. Alexander. It was a three-story Italianate marble structure that featured a four-story central clock tower, complete with a crenelated roofline. It sat on what was a former summer estate of George W. Riggs, surrounded by 225 lush acres of pasture, orchards, and open fields.

Funds for the construction and four additional building came from a tax imposed on Mexico City during the Mexican War. A sum of $118,000 was raised, with an additional $54,000 added by the government that had been targeted to return disabled veterans to their homes. General Winfield Scott was the force behind the idea of the Soldiers' Home, and the original building was named after him.

Incredibly, just 11 years after it had been completed, Scott Hall was transformed into a Second Empire-style building with the addition of a third story under a Mansard roof, and a Mansard cap on the clock tower. Two large rear additions in 1884 and 1887 were designed by Capt. Scott W. Davis to house an additional 1,200 veterans.

The additions had been designed in the Gothic Revival style, and the decision was made to remodel Scott Hall once again, in 1890, to match the additions.

Scott Hall was renamed Sherman Hall in 1954 when a modern dormitory was constructed and named after General Scott. In the 1960s nearly 40

SOLDIERS' LAST STAND

Two other original and significant buildings at the U.S. Soldiers' Home have been razed. One included the fantastic Stick-styled Victorian library, with wrap around porch and polychromatic slate roof. It was built in 1877 and designed by the Smithmyer and Peltz architectural firm. Its high cost of maintenance contributed to the decision to have it razed a short time later, in 1910. The other lost building on the campus was Sheridan Hall that had been built in the Second Empire style in 1885. It was built with a two-story, cast-iron porch, named after General Philip H. Sheridan, who was involved in the formation of the U.S. Soldiers' Home.

percent of the campus was sold to build the Washington Hospital Center and the Veterans' Administration Hospital. Irving Street and North Capitol Street were cut through the property at this time.

Today, the campus is known as the U.S. Soldiers' and Airmen's Home, welcoming both male and female veterans from the armed services.

LEFT *The remodeled Scott Hall, with the 1868 addition of a third floor and Mansard roof on the clock tower.*

RIGHT *In 1890, Scott Hall was once again remodeled, this time as a Gothic Revival-style building. Lincoln's Cottage is visible on the left.*

Freedman's Savings Bank RAZED 1899

The idea for a permanent bank serving the immediate needs for hundreds of thousands of freed blacks following the Civil War was first comprehended by a white Congregational minister named John W. Alford. In early 1865, he was serving as the chaplain in Union General Sherman's army in Savannah, Georgia. Perhaps it was his witnessing of Sherman's burning of that city and many others in the South that prompted Alford to approach Congress to pass a bill establishing the Freedman's Savings Bank in March of 1865.

ABOVE *Frederick Douglass served on the Board of Directors of Freedman's Savings Bank from 1874.*

RIGHT *Union General Nathaniel P. Banks (1816–94) established a series of temporary banks for freed blacks and black soldiers during the Civil War.*

LEFT *A circa-1890 photograph of Freedman's Saving Bank at 1509 Pennsylvania Avenue, NW.*

A series of three temporary Freedman's banks had been established earlier on army posts in Beaufort, South Carolina, New Orleans, Louisiana, and Norfolk, Virginia in 1864 by the aptly named Union General Nathaniel P. Banks. They were created to protect the earned cash of black soldiers and freed blacks who were susceptible to losing money from theft and dishonest post traders.

John Alford was appointed temporary president of his bank, and with the close of the Civil War, its headquarters were established in New York City. From there, Alford established a total of 32 branches, mostly in southern states. It was separate from the Freedman's Bureau, a relief agency aiming to establish hospitals, schools, and food disbursement camps to the formerly enslaved.

The headquarters moved to Washington, D.C., in 1868, and its officers hired the architectural firm of Nathan G. Starkweather and Thomas M. Plowman to design their French Mansard-styled building, erected the following year. It faced Jackson Square, and was located on the corner of Pennsylvania Avenue and Madison Place, opposite the White House. It was built of Hummelstown Brownstone at a cost of a staggering $260,000.

Just eight years after it was established, Freedman's Savings Bank was a huge success: it had 72,000 depositors and $57 million in cash.

However, many of the managers and cashiers had been appointed rather than hired for their experience, and that amount of cash was irresistible to corrupt employees. Bad loans were lent, and records were poorly kept, if at all. Conditions worsened beginning with the economic depression of 1873.

That was all news to noted abolitionist Frederick Douglass, whom Alford had recruited to become the bank's executive head. In his autobiography, Douglass described the first few months of his tenure at the institution as thus:

> … one of the most costly and splendid buildings of the time, finished on the inside with black walnut and furnished with marble counters and all modern improvements … I was amazed with the facility with which they counted the money. They threw off thousands with the dexterity, if not the accuracy, of old experienced clerks. The whole thing was beautiful.

To his shock, the bank was forced into bankruptcy just three months after Douglass joined its Board of Directors in 1874. Thousands of black account holders lost their life savings. The bank was placed under Federal control, perhaps foreshadowing the similar event amongst Wall Street banks 135 years later.

The Federal government bought the building in 1882 for $250,000. It was used for various federal offices, including the Department of Justice, until it was razed in 1899. The site sat vacant until the Treasury annex was built there between 1918 and 1919.

Mills Foundry RAZED CIRCA 1900

About 1860, a Syracuse, New York native sculptor named Clark Mills built a large octagonal foundry at the edge of the city at 2530 Bladensburg Road, NE. His background was surprising: an impoverished orphan, Mills made his way to Charleston, South Carolina where he found work as a house plasterer. He also studied sculpture, and was soon a master at creating busts of wealthy citizens.

With members of Congress supporting his trade, he entered and won a competition in 1848 for a large equestrian statue of Andrew Jackson in Lafayette Square, Washington. The exquisite result, Jackson on a rearing horse standing on just two feet, won him much praise. Weighing 15 tons, Mills had cast it in a temporary foundry near the site. It was dedicated on January 8, 1853.

With his profits he bought a farm on Bladensburg Road, where he built a house and his octagonal foundry. He was commissioned to create three more statues for New Orleans, Nashville, and the Washington Statue in Washington Circle in the city. He enlisted the help of his mixed-race slave Philip Reid, whom he paid to work on Sundays.

Mills accepted delivery of an ornate plaster mold sculpted by American Thomas Crawford in 1859. Called the *Statue of Freedom*, the 19.5-foot tall mold had previously been exhibited, calling for its five major sections to be smoothed over with plaster. After an artist in Mills' employ refused to reveal where the sections would come apart without a significant pay rise, the enslaved Reid stepped in and solved the mystery. The mold was successfully disassembled using a pulley and tackle.

Reid continued to work on the difficult casting of such a large piece. Perhaps fitting given the name of the artwork, Reid found himself a free man when President Lincoln ordered the city's enslaved free on April 16, 1862 through paid emancipation.

Reid became an employee of the Mills foundry, and worked there when the 15,000-pound *Statue of Freedom* was hoisted atop the U.S. Capitol Dome on December 2, 1863. It was celebrated with a 35-gun salute, one for each state at that time, including those in the Confederacy. Mills died in 1883, and his foundry was razed circa 1900.

THE EARLIER EMANCIPATION PROCLAMATION

While the slave trade was prohibited in Washington in 1850, enslaved persons were a common occurrence in the city, especially with wealthy residents or Congressmen. Older hotels maintained slave pens for their guests to ensure the security of their slaves in a city that was also abundant with freed blacks. A full nine months before his famous nationwide Emancipation Proclamation (see page 10), on April 16, 1862, President Lincoln signed into law a paid emancipation bill that provided money to Washington, D.C. resident slave owners. Owners were paid up to $300 for each enslaved person, as long as the owner was loyal to the Union, and up to $100 to each freed slave if they chose to emigrate from the United States. Over the next nine months, the federal government paid nearly $1 million for approximately 3,100 former slaves in the city. The date is still celebrated in annual festivities among the city residents. On January 1, 1863, Lincoln's Emancipation Proclamation freed slaves in the Confederate states.

Navy Yard Ship Houses RAZED CIRCA 1901

The Washington Navy Yard was established at the foot of 8th Street, SE in 1799. It was built as a cost-saving measure to have naval ships constructed at government-owned facilities instead of private shipyards. Benjamin Stoddert was the first Secretary of the Department of the Navy when it was established in 1798; Captain Thomas Tingey built the Navy Yard beginning in 1800.

Tingey first built a brick fence and guard towers around the property, and architect Benjamin Henry Latrobe designed the main gate, commandant's house, and workshops. The facility's first mission was to mothball several wooden sailing ships in the Navy's fleet that included the *Constitution*, *United States*, and the *Constellation*.

The manufacture of new warships was authorized by Congress shortly thereafter, in response to the seizure of American merchant ships by the French, Spanish, and British navies. The first ship built at the Navy Yard was the *Wasp*, and it proved far superior to the Navy's older fleet.

Tingey was ordered to destroy the Navy Yard before the British could seize supplies and ammunition stored there. This followed the British success at the Battle of Bladensburg and their subsequent occupation of Washington in August of 1814. The Navy Yard was rebuilt in 1815 and began the manufacture of ships supplies, including chains for new warships.

Commodore John Rodgers recommended building a ship house at the Navy Yard in 1822 to facilitate a quicker turnaround and fewer fatalities in construction and refurbishment. The resulting buildings dominated the skyline for decades to come, often depicted in early engravings. They stood seven stories high and were 300 feet long.

Rodgers had also created a new technique to haul ships out of the water and into the building using iron rails, a series of pulleys, and an inclined rail system. The first ship to be built at the Navy Yard was the *Potomac*. By the 1840s, the Navy Yard was producing steam operated ships for the Navy fleet, which could operate in shallow waters and small rivers, and most importantly, outrun a sailing vessel. The *Minnesota* was launched at the Navy yard in 1854. At 243 feet in length, it was considered one of the largest steamships in the world.

By the outbreak of the Civil War in 1861, the naval fleet numbered 700 warships. Just prior to the war, the Navy Yard expanded to include the manufacture and perfection of large-caliber cannon and guns. This continued into the 1880s and 1890s, and by 1892 the workforce increased from 300 to 1,000.

The conversion from wood to steel warships during the Spanish American War in 1898 meant that the ship building houses became quickly obsolete. Development and construction along the upper reaches of the Anacostia River resulted in silting and shallow water, with expensive dredging required to keep shipping lanes open. No longer needed in the manufacture of tall wooden ships, the Navy Yard's two main buildings were razed circa 1901. The iron rails, however, can still be seen slipping into the Anacostia River at the shore edge.

ABOVE *Tens of thousands of Washington residents have worked at the Navy Yard, assembling weapons, refurbishing cannon, and casting guns.*

LEFT *This illustration of the Navy Yard Ship Houses appeared in* Harper's Weekly *on April 20, 1861.*

RIGHT *The slanted walls demonstrate the size of the buildings; skylights provided ventilation and natural light.*

Columbian College Campus RELOCATED 1904

Construction of the first building for Columbian College, now The George Washington University, was completed in 1822 on a new campus bounded by Columbia Road, 13th, 14th, and Boundary Street (now Florida Avenue). Two houses were also built for professors that year. The area was then surrounded by farms and orchards at the edge of the city, although small suburban developments had begun sprouting up close by. The land itself cost a mere $6,988.

President George Washington expressed in his will in 1799 that his "ardent wish" was for a university to be established within the city. He wanted a place "to which the youth of fortune and talent from all parts [of the country] might be sent for the completion of their education in all the branches of polite literature, in arts and sciences, in acquiring knowledge in the principles of politics and good government." He also left a bequest toward that objective.

President James Monroe and 32 members of the U.S. Congress created an Act of Congress that was signed by the President on February 9, 1821, creating the Columbian College in the District of Columbia, a private, nonsectarian institution. The following year, Columbian College opened its doors with three faculty members, one tutor and 30 students in a single building. The campus was known as College Hill.

The school's curriculum included English, Latin and Greek, as well as mathematics, chemistry, astronomy, reading, writing, navigation and political law. The first graduates received their degrees in December of 1824. Shortly after, Columbian College added a medical school and a law school.

By the time the Civil War broke out, the school had expanded into several buildings on the hill overlooking the capital. Like many institutions, its buildings were commandeered for use of a hospital and barracks. Walt Whitman was among the war volunteers on the campus.

In 1873, Columbian College changed its name to Columbian University and opened additional buildings downtown at 15th and H Streets, NW. It began offering doctoral degrees and admitted its first women.

In 1903, the institution purchased the Van Ness mansion and its surroundings at 17th Street and Constitution Avenue, NW for $161,000 in the hopes of moving out of their cramped building at 15th and H Streets, NW (see Van Ness Mansion, page 37). The prestigious firm of Hornblower & Marshall drew up elaborate plans for a complete college campus, but it was never constructed. At the time, the institution had 1,200 students.

The site was a crucial aspect for a deal with the George Washington Memorial Association that had originally been formed to honor Washington's request for a university in the nation's capital. That entity suggested renaming Columbian University to The George Washington University, and they had the leverage for the change; the group would completely fund the new campus on the Van Ness site. In the meantime, however, the school's Board of Trustees was weary of the nearby diseased Washington City Canal, and subsequently sold the property in 1907. It was a costly decision, as the Memorial group then rescinded its offer to pay for the campus.

The College moved from its Meridian Hill location to various buildings downtown, until it purchased a building at 2023 G Street, NW in 1912. With the insistence of Board member and G Street resident General Maxwell van Zandt Woodhull, the University later expanded to dozens of blocks in the Foggy Bottom neighborhood where it remains to this day.

The federal government also purchased a large portion of the college's land in Columbia Heights and built Meridian Hill Park in the early 20th century.

OPPOSITE PAGE *The main Columbian College building can be seen behind the rows of hospital tents at Camp Carver in this photograph from May 1864.*

BELOW LEFT *The 16th Street retaining wall of Meridian Hill Park (unofficially known as Malcolm X Park) is shown under construction in this 1912 photograph.*

BELOW *J. C. Welling, President of Columbian University (now The George Washington University), photographed circa 1871.*

Washington Arsenal BURNED 1814, RAZED BETWEEN 1903 AND 1907

The site of the Washington Arsenal is one of the oldest continually used army installations in the country today. Located on the point where the Potomac and Anacostia rivers conjoin, the site was an obvious choice for city planner Pierre L'Enfant to select for a military fort in 1792. It was named Greenleaf point after James Greenleaf, a Bostonian real estate speculator that had purchased much of the surrounding land anticipating large rewards as the city began to take shape in the 1790s.

President Jefferson approved a plan for the arsenal building created by George Hadfield. It was soon utilized as a distribution center for munitions, rifles, and cannon manufactured in earlier established arsenals in the colonies.

On August 24, 1814 following the successful Battle of Bladensburg, the invading British Army entered the city with 200 troops. Before they could take control of the precious arsenal and its munitions, the commander there burned the building, and secretly hid a large amount of gunpowder in a dry well. The British team who

lowered a lantern into the well to search for munitions got what they were looking for: the light sparked a huge explosion, killing 12 soldiers and injuring 30 more.

The arsenal was rebuilt in 1816, and in 1822 a series of eight Federal-style buildings were added to the site. Just outside the northern gate, the city penitentiary was built in 1826, constructed to the designs of Charles Bulfinch, much to the consternation of the army. By the late 1830s, the arsenal had been described as holding an impressive 800 cannons, 30 brass cannon, howitzers, 40,000 rifles, and 100 cannon carriages that had been made on site. It was also producing shells and shot.

During the final stages of the Civil War in June of 1864, another explosion hit the arsenal, this time killing 21 women and injuring dozens of others. A firework had been laid out to dry in the sun, ignited, and flew through an open window where the women were assembling rifle carriages. The communal funeral possession was led by President

Lincoln, and the deceased were buried in a mass grave at Congressional Cemetery on Capitol Hill.

Used for training purposes, hundreds of tiny models of weapons used in all previous wars were relocated to the arsenal following the Civil War. As needs changed, the arsenal was transformed into a barracks in 1881, and many of its buildings used for the storage of uniforms and supplies.

The arsenal was pressed into service again during the Spanish-American War, when a small hospital was built on the site in 1898.

The site was later chosen to house a new Army War College and was built on the site following the razing of approximately 90 percent of the original buildings between 1903 and 1907. The Army War College continues to operate as the National Defense University today.

ABOVE *The elegant architecture of the Washington Arsenal often hid dangerous working conditions.*

LEFT *The arsenal yard with the Potomac River behind.*

RIGHT *A Civil War-era photograph of guns and equipment of the Excelsior Brigade at the Washington Arsenal.*

Van Ness Mansion RAZED 1908

John Peter Van Ness (1770–1846) had his mansion built on the block bounded by Constitution Avenue, C, 17th, and Eighth Streets, NW just steps away from the White House beginning in 1813. It was considered one of the finest residences in the city when he and his wife moved in in 1816. It was designed by Benjamin Henry Latrobe in an early Greek Revival style.

Visitors gained entrance to the house via two porters' houses at the southwest corner of 17th and C Streets, NW. Van Ness arrived in the new city of Washington in 1801 as a New York House of Representative member from Kinderhook, New York. His modest fortune blossomed when he met and married Miss Marcia Burnes (1782–1832) in Washington, D.C. in 1802. As it turns out, she was the sole heir to 600 acres of land that had been included in the plan for central Washington, valued at an astonishing $1.5 million. She was the wealthiest woman in the city.

Her father, David Burnes Jr., had expanded a farm originally purchased in 1721 by his father, a Scottish immigrant, into what today is bounded by Constitution Avenue, H, Third, and 18th Streets, NW. The Burnes family lived in a typical wood-frame house at what would become 17th Street and Constitutional Avenue, NW, which was preserved by Marcia Burnes after they built their mansion next door. It remained until 1894, when it was razed for an athletic field. Barnes reluctantly sold portions of

the land in 1792 for the formation of Washington, although he continued to plant tobacco in the laid out streets for decades to come.

President Jefferson appointed Van Ness that same year as a major in the city militia, then part of the federal government. That was technically a violation of the Constitution, as pointed out by a number of his opposing Federalist Party congressmen, and they had him removed from his Congressional seat in 1803. No member of Congress could hold a position in the federal government. Van Ness and his wife stayed in Washington, however. He later became a major general in the District of Columbia militia in 1813.

Van Ness became president of the Bank of the Metropolis in 1814. It was considered the second largest bank in Washington at the time it was established, and would quickly grow to become the largest. Van Ness purchased the Rhodes Tavern at 15th and F Streets, NW as its first location (see page 135). He was also founder of the Saint John's Episcopal Church on Lafayette Square, and was eventually elected as Mayor of Washington, serving from 1830 to 1834. Their house became the social center of Washington with elaborate parties held for government officials and visiting dignitaries.

Marcia Van Ness graciously funded and founded the Washington City Orphan Asylum in 1815. It was created to care for the destitute children of soldiers injured or killed in the War of 1812. She donated a vacant lot on H Street between Ninth and 10th Streets, NW, where their building was constructed in 1828.

The house was sold by Trustees after John Peter Van Ness's death in 1846 to a prominent newspaperman named Thomas Green. However, when the Washington City Canal began to deteriorate after being used as a sewer during the Civil War—it was in the mansion's back yard—the house was abandoned as a residence. Ironically, Van Ness himself had served as the president of the commissioners of the Washington City Canal in 1834. The mansion's former gracious rooms were later used as a German beer garden, florist and nursery, an office for the city street cleaners, and finally as the Columbian Athletic Club.

The mansion and land were purchased for the hopeful site of the new Columbian College campus

in 1902, but that plan never materialized (see page 33). Instead, the institution sold the mansion in 1907 for $200,000 to the federal government. The State Department had plans for a "Bureau of American Republics" that eventually resulted in the construction of the Pan American Union Building on the site today.

ABOVE *The only known image of John Peter Van Ness (1770–1846), in a daguerreotype by noted photographer Matthew B. Brady.*

LEFT *The Van Ness Mansion in disrepair, shortly before it was razed in 1908.*

OPPOSITE PAGE *An unidentified man in top hat and coat poses in front of the Van Ness Mansion at 17th Street and Constitution Avenue, NW.*

Baltimore & Potomac Railroad Station

RAZED 1908

It took five years to build, but Washingtonians were no doubt delighted with the results of the new Baltimore and Potomac Railroad Station when it opened in 1878. The massive building was located at Constitution Avenue and Sixth Street, NW. It was designed by Joseph Miller Wilson, who included a 130-foot train shed that extended half way across the National Mall. The B&P operated from Baltimore, Maryland, southwest to Washington, D.C., between 1872 and 1902. The company was controlled by the Pennsylvania Railroad.

Early train travel in Washington was not as sophisticated as in other cities like New York. In fact, it wasn't until 1852 that whole trains were allowed to cross the city. Prior to that, the steam engines were considered too dangerous and were separated from the passenger and luggage compartments outside the city, and the train was pulled in by a team of horses.

The first train station was a converted house at the corner of Pennsylvania Avenue and Second Street, NW for the Baltimore & Ohio Railroad. That was replaced by a new B&O Railroad station constructed at New Jersey Avenue and C Street, NW in 1852, welcoming both engines and passenger cars.

Following the Civil War, a second wooden platform and simple station that would greet trains coming from the south was erected where the B&P Station was eventually built from 1873 to 1878. Tracks ran south from the station along Sixth Street to a wye junction at Sixth Street SW, Maryland Avenue SW, and Virginia Avenue SW. (Somewhat confusingly, the tracks along Maryland Avenue ran over the Long Bridge to Virginia.) The problem remained, however, in transferring passengers and large amounts of luggage from one station to the other that were connecting through Washington.

The McMillan Commission solved that problem when it insisted on razing all Victorian structures facing the National Mall just after the turn of the 20th century. Union Station was commissioned and opened in 1907 at Massachusetts Avenue and North Capitol Street, serving several railroads. A year later, both the B&P and B&O stations were razed. The site of the B&P Station is now occupied by the West Building of the National Gallery of Art.

B&P STATION MAKES FRONT-PAGE NEWS

The Baltimore & Potomac Station will forever be remembered for the attempted assassination of President James A. Garfield. He was shot at 9:30 a.m. on Saturday, July 2, 1881 by Charles J. Guiteau. He had blamed the President for his unsuccessful attempt at getting himself appointed a federal job. Garfield was taken to the White House, where doctors failed to locate the remains of the bullet. He was transferred by train for recuperation in Elberton, New Jersey, where he died of his wounds on September 19, 1881.

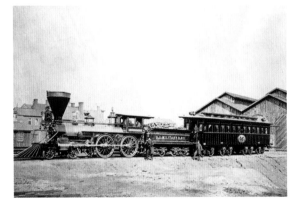

ABOVE *An illustration of the attempted assassination of President Garfield from* Frank Leslie's Illustrated Newspaper, *July 16, 1881.*

FAR LEFT *The rear train yards behind the B&P Station.*

LEFT *The train carrying President Abraham Lincoln's casket awaits departure from the rival B&O Station on Capitol Hill.*

RIGHT *An early 1900s view of the old station. Today the site is occupied by the West Building of the National Gallery of Art.*

No. 222.—MARYLAND AVENUE DEPOT, WASHINGTON, D. C.,
June, 1863.

Maryland Avenue Railroad Yard and Tracks

REMOVED 1908

During the early onset of the Civil War, the Baltimore and Ohio Railroad (B & O) constructed a rail yard along Maryland Avenue, NE for the purpose of protecting their locomotives and trains from Confederate capture. It was connected by rail to the B&O Station, then located on New Jersey Avenue and C Streets, NW.

B&O was one of the oldest railroads in the United States and the first common carrier railroad. It was established when the city of Baltimore wanted to compete with the newly constructed Erie Canal and another canal being proposed in Pennsylvania. A grand station with clock tower was built in 1852, having been designed by the Niernsee & Neilson architectural firm.

At the outset of the Civil War, B&O possessed 236 locomotives, 128 passenger coaches, 3,451 rail cars and 513 miles of track, all in states south of the Mason-Dixon Line. B&O was instrumental in supporting the Federal government during the Civil War, as it was the main rail connection between Washington, D.C., and the northern states. As a result, 143 raids and battles during the war involved the B&O Railroad, many resulting in substantial loss.

Years after the Civil War ended in 1865 and the Maryland Avenue Rail Yard was to have been dismantled, it remaining in full use by B&O, mostly due to political connections. That came to a brief end in 1872, when Alexander R. "Boss" Shepherd had the tracks disconnected one night, severing the tie between the station and the Long Bridge (see page 13). His bold statement was part of his reign as the head of the D.C. Board of Public Works to drastically improve the city's infrastructure and street aesthetics.

Railroad tracks placed down the center of the city's streets were a constant threat to pedestrians, horses, and their carriages. More than 30 people were maimed or killed per year. The tracks were reconnected, however, and remained in place until Union Station was opened in 1908.

ABOVE *Trains making their way across city streets were a constant threat to pedestrians, animals, and vehicles alike.*

OPPOSITE PAGE *Before townhouses lined Maryland Avenue, NE, there was a vast rail yard for the B&O Railroad.*

Noble House RAZED 1915

Belden Noble (1810–81) built the impressive and fanciful brick mansion at 17th Street and Massachusetts Avenue beginning in June of 1880. Designed by the architectural firm of Gray & Page, it was constructed at a cost of $50,000, at a time when the typical Washington rowhouse was being built for $2,500. Noble, a native of Essex, New York, didn't have much time to enjoy his new mansion; on July 15, 1881, he drowned while fishing along the shallow shores of Lake Champlain.

Harper's Magazine made mention of the Noble house in 1882, stating that it was "perhaps the best illustration in the city of what might be accomplished in massiveness and the ornament in brick, without superficial adornment. It is 13th-century Gothic in its general effect. His widow, the former Adeline M. Ferris (1831–1910), lived at the mansion during the winter with her son William and daughter Mary Maud, while summering in Essex, New York.

The mansion was sold in 1906 to Stanley McCormick (1875–1947) of Chicago. McCormick had inherited his family business, the McCormick Harvesting Machine Company—a machinery, construction equipment, vehicle, commercial truck, and household and commercial products manufacturer. In 1902, J.P. Morgan merged the company with the Deering Harvester Company, along with three smaller agricultural equipment firms, to form the giant behemoth International Harvester.

McCormick rented the residence to William H. Moody (1853–1917), a politician and jurist who held positions in all three branches of the U.S. government. After appointment as the U.S. Attorney for Eastern Massachusetts in 1890, he gained

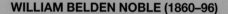

WILLIAM BELDEN NOBLE (1860–96)

The William Belden Noble Lectures at Harvard University were named after Belden Noble's son. He was a member of the Harvard Class of 1885 and attended the Episcopal Theological School at Harvard in 1888 before his declining health interrupted his studies. He died in 1896 while seeking relief in the mountains of Colorado. The popular lecture series was established two years later by his widow, Nannie Yulee Noble. According to the terms of the bequest: "The object of the Founder of the Lectures is to continue the mission of her husband, whose supreme desire was to extend the influence of Jesus as 'the Way, the Truth, and the Life.'"

widespread notoriety in 1893 as the junior prosecutor in the Lizzie Borden murder case. Moody served as the Secretary of the Navy from 1902 to 1904, and Attorney General from 1904 to 1906. He was appointed a U.S. Supreme Court Justice on December 17, 1906.

Stanley McCormick was declared incompetent in 1909 after suffering years of mental illness. His guardians razed the Noble mansion in 1915 and replaced it with the McCormick Apartment House, designed by Jules Henry de Sibour. It featured a single vast apartment on each floor, and is considered the finest apartment building ever constructed in the city. Today it is the headquarters for the National Trust for Historic Preservation.

LEFT *Supreme Court Justice William H. Moody, who rented Noble House from Stanley McCormick.*

OPPOSITE PAGE *The Noble House at 17th Street and Massachusetts Avenue, built in 1880. The site is now occupied by the National Trust for Historic Preservation.*

Belmont Castle RAZED 1915

Asphalt remains the most common paving material in the United States, and most motorists don't give it a second thought unless confronted with a pothole or paving project that slows down a commute. And few motorists descending the steep grade down 14th Street from Columbia Heights are likely aware that Washington resident Amzi L. Barber (1843–1909) was known as America's "King of Asphalt" and lived in a lavish stone mansion at 14th Street and Clifton Street overlooking the city. He was also an early real estate developer and one of the earliest automobile manufacturers in America.

Amzi Lorenzo Barber was born in Saxton's River, Vermont on June 22, 1843, graduated from Oberlin College in 1867. He came to Washington in April of 1868 to work as director and professor at Howard University, by the invitation of General Otis O. Howard. That same year, he married Celia M. Bradley of Geneva, Ohio, who died just two years later. In 1871, Barber married Julia Louise Langdon, the daughter of successful real estate broker J. LeDroict Langdon and resigned his post at Howard the following year.

By 1872, Barber had formed a new real estate development company with his new brother-in-law, Andrew Langdon, having conveniently purchased 40 acres of land from Howard University for $50,000. He used this land to develop LeDroit Park, named after his father-in-law's middle name, albeit without the original awkward 'c.'

LeDroit Park was developed as an exclusively white residential area, enforced by a wrought iron fence erected to surround the community, most of which was designed by architect James H. McGill. The fence became a focal point of unrest, and in July of 1888, it was torn down by protesting African Americans, which signaled a movement toward the integration of the area. In 1893, a barber, Octavius Williams, became the first African American to move into the subdivision.

Barber became interested in the laying of Trinidad sheet asphalt in 1878, and formed the Barber Asphalt Company in 1882; it expanded substantially over the next decade and was awarded contracts to pave streets by municipalities all over the nation and in Europe. In fact, it provided nearly 50 percent of all asphalt pavements laid in the United States by 1896.

He attempted to squash all competition by establishing a trust in 1899 that sold $30 million's worth of shares, and Barber went into semi-retirement in London, England. An avid yachtsman, Barber launched the 300-foot steamer *Lorena* on January 14, 1903, named after his daughter. He went on to purchase the $500,000 Robert Stewart mansion in Manhattan and the Cunard estate on Staten Island.

In 1880, Barber and Senator John Sherman purchased and developed the 120-acre Stone estate, today composing much of the Columbia Heights neighborhood. He reserved the land above Florida Avenue, between 13th and 14th Streets to Clifton Street, for his own estate, where he commissioned Philadelphia architect Theophilus P. Chandler in 1886 to design a large stone Chateauesque Queen Anne mansion on the expansive grounds. Its grand scale and tall dormered tower made it one of Washington's most imposing mansions. Barber named it Belmont, most likely after Belmont, New York, where his father-in-law hailed from.

Perhaps a natural business expansion to the asphalt industry was Barber's entry into the automobile industry. One of the first automobiles produced was coined the "Locomobile," created by brothers Francis and Freelan Stanley in 1898. But only a few months into their venture, they sold their enterprise to Barber. It was under his direction that the Locomobile name became a brand; the 1899 Locomobile sold for $600 and was advertised as both noiseless and odorless. Sales of the Locomobile peaked in 1900 at 1,600 units, a remarkable figure nearly a decade before Ford streamlined the assembly line.

Barber's successful ventures as a businessman didn't always go smoothly, however. In January of 1898, a court in New York awarded a former business partner $700,000 and interest in any future profits. General W.W. Averill had formed the American Asphalt Company with Barber in 1881, but Barber folded that company and formed his own a year later, and continued to use the same processes he learned from Averill.

Following his death in 1909, his widow and son LeDroit Barber continued to live at Belmont until its contents were sold in the spring of 1914. LeDroit had the house razed a year later to make way for his own large-scale real estate development, known as the Clifton Terrace apartment complex. Belmont Street was laid out on the southern portion of the property, the only remaining reference to the once-grand Belmont estate.

LEFT *The lavish Victorian interiors of Belmont Castle.*

RIGHT *The imposing residence was home to the "King of Asphalt," Amzi L. Barber.*

Commercial Traffic on the C&O Canal

CEASED 1924

Mercantile traffic on the Chesapeake and Ohio (C&O) Canal operated from 1831 until 1924. The canal ran parallel to the Potomac River, from Cumberland, Maryland to Washington, D.C. for a total of 184.5 miles. The elevation change of 605 feet was accommodated with a total of 74 canal locks, and the crossing of major streams and rivers required the construction of 11 aqueducts. The canal also extends through the 3,118-foot Paw Paw Tunnel.

George Washington himself was the chief advocate of using man-made waterways to connect the Eastern Seaboard to the Great Lakes and the Ohio River. He founded the Potowmack Company in 1785 to make navigability improvements to the Potomac River by building a number of skirting canals around the major falls.

In 1824, the holdings of the Potowmack Company were ceded to the Chesapeake and Ohio Company. Construction of the C&O Canal began with a groundbreaking ceremony on July 4, 1828 by President John Quincy Adams. The canal initially connected to the Potomac River on the east side of Georgetown by joining Rock Creek, and its first section opened in 1831 from Georgetown to Seneca, Maryland. In 1833 the canal opened to Harpers Ferry, and at the Georgetown end it was extended 1.5 miles eastward to Tiber Creek, near the western terminus of the Washington City Canal. A lock keeper's house remains to this day at the southwest corner of Constitution Avenue and 17th Street, NW.

The C&O Canal was used for the carriage of U.S. mail, with a $1,000 yearly contract given in 1836 to Albert Humrickhouse for services between Georgetown and Shepherdstown, West Virginia. It also transported tobacco and other agricultural products in a series of specially made canal boats, towed along the length by a team of horses walking along an adjacent towpath. By the time the canal reached Cumberland, Maryland in 1850, it had already been rendered somewhat obsolete; the B&O Railroad had reached Cumberland eight years previously. Debt-ridden, the company dropped its plan to continue construction of the next 180 miles of the canal into the Ohio River Valley.

The canal continued to carry an impressive amount of agricultural goods, however, and added coal mined in West Virginia. In the 1870s, a canal-inclined plane was built two miles upriver from Georgetown so that boats could bypass the congestion in Georgetown. The inclined plane was dismantled after a major flood in 1889. That same year, the ownership of the canal was purchased by the B&O Railroad to prevent its right of way falling into the hands of the Western Maryland Railway.

Commercial transport ceased in 1924 after a flood damaged the canal beyond reasonable repair. In 1938, the abandoned canal was obtained by the federal government in a land exchange with the B&O Railroad. By the 1950s, an effort was thwarted to transform the canal into an automobile parkway, and it was eventually transferred to the National Park Service who maintains the canal as a recreational park today.

ABOVE *Swimmers enjoy the cool water during summer.*

RIGHT *A towboat is led under the Wisconsin Avenue Bridge in Georgetown by a guide and two horses.*

BELOW *Towboats docked along the canal in 1925, after commercial traffic ceased.*

Semaphore Traffic Signal DISCONTINUED CIRCA 1925

Tragically, 10-year-old Marion Kahlert became Washington's first traffic fatality, when she was struck by an automobile in 1904. Like other cities, Washington was experiencing a new method of transportation with the introduction of the automobile that often collided, quite literally, with each other, and with curbs, houses, telephone poles, horses, and pedestrians.

The invasion of the automobile in America went from just 460,000 vehicles in 1910 to an astounding eight million in 1920. A particular problem for Washington was its intersections, which had no signals to direct traffic from each approaching street. The free-for-all that had worked for the pace of a horse was proving itself to be impossible for motorized vehicles.

Police officers were placed at the most dangerous intersections, and they used a system of hand pointing and whistle blows in an attempt to direct traffic. About 1915, the city began to use a semaphore—a pole with an umbrella affixed on top to protect the police officer and four painted signs that read simply "stop" and "go." The officer would sound a horn shortly before he would spin the pole around to alert automobile traffic that one direction was ordered to stop. They were first used in Toledo, Ohio, about 1908.

Early attempts at replacing the human element with an automatic electrical signal had various rates of success. It was William Potts of the Detroit Police Department that first installed in 1920 the three signal lights with the now familiar red, yellow and green lights. The color of the traffic lights representing stop and go are thought to be derived from those used to identify port (red) and starboard (green) in maritime rules governing right of way, where the vessel on the left must stop for the one crossing on the right.

The use of hand-held traffic signaling was eventually fazed out circa 1925.

LEFT AND FAR RIGHT *These photographs from 1913 show the hand-turned signal at 14th Street and Pennsylvania Avenue, NW.*

RIGHT *This switch tower was built for the complex intersections at Union Plaza in front of Union Station. This circa-1940 photo shows it after it relocated to 14th Street and New York Avenue, NW.*

MAKING THE SWITCH

The opening of Union Station in 1908 resulted in a flurry of streetcar traffic headed into and out of this new major transportation hub. As a preventative measure, several streetcar companies came together to pay for and erect a series of five switch towers at intersections along Union Plaza. The switchman was housed atop an eight-foot pole, enabling him to view oncoming streetcars from three blocks away. He could then judge which one would approach the intersection first, and switch the tracks for a turn. Streetcars knew the tracks were in their favor by a green light mounted in the street. The towers were relocated to other critical intersections after it was found that the Union Plaza's configuration was adequate for non-supervised switching. The tower pictured left was relocated to 14th Street and New York Avenue, NW in about 1940. They were removed after automated switching technology no longer required human supervision.

Washington Bathing Beach CLOSED CIRCA 1925

Washington residents had their own Potomac bathing beach beginning in the 1890s that was located in the Tidal Basin, where the Jefferson Memorial is now situated. Changing rooms and lockers for valuables were located on the shore, and every summer a huge floating raft was brought to the site which had diving boards and a slide. The local newspapers included many photographs of the annual bathing suit contest, which was watched by thousands of spectators. The first annual contest, held on July 27, 1919, attracted more than 5,000 spectators. Mrs. Audrey O'Connor was proclaimed by the judges as Washington's most beautiful girl in a bathing suit, while first prize in the costume contest was awarded to Mrs. Grace Fleishman. Silver loving cups were awarded to the winners.

But it wasn't all fun and games. *The Washington Post* included a list of rules for the bathing beach on September 5, 1918:

> The public buildings and grounds has announced the following rules for the new bathing beach on the shore of the Tidal Basin in Potomac Park:
> Bathing hours—7 a. m. to 12 m.;
> 2 p. m. to 7 p. m.
> Open daily, including Sunday and holidays.
> Bathing suits rented, 25 cents for men and 35 cents for women.
> A charge will be made for soap, towels and checking valuables.
> No children under six years of age allowed to bathe unless accompanied by adult member of the family.

Floating debris was becoming a health hazard by 1925, when it was being operated by the newly merged Office of Public Buildings and Grounds and Office of Public Parks of the National Capital. The bathing beach was restricted to whites only and pressure to open up the beach to black residents was rebuffed. The beach was closed circa 1925 and the former site of the bathing beach was filled in with the beginning of construction for the Jefferson Memorial in 1939. The memorial was completed in 1943.

ABOVE *Washington policeman Bill Norton is pictured on June 30, 1922, measuring the distance between knee and suit at the bathing beach. Col. Sherrill, Superintendent of Public Buildings and Grounds, had issued an order that suits not be over six inches above the knee.*

LEFT *Yearly "bathing beauties" contest and parades were held at the beach, with women competing in their finest swimming attire. These beauties were photographed on July 26, 1919.*

RIGHT *Before the Potomac River became polluted and unfit for swimming, it was the site of a popular bathing beach. The 555-foot Washington Monument is seen behind.*

Krazy Kat Klub DISMANTLED 1925

A bohemian club located just steps away from Thomas Circle in the teens and 1920s must have been an unusual sight to behold for those lucky enough to locate its entrance and know about its whereabouts. It was located in an alley at 3 Green Court, across from what is today's Green Lantern bar. It was coined the Krazy Kat.

The club's entrance was along the side of the Green Lantern building, leading to Massachusetts Avenue, with a small sign that read "Syne of ye Krazy Kat." A warning on the door read "All soap abandon ye who enter here." Inside, patrons found a tree house reached by a precarious ladder, pebble floor, and al fresco dining. It was the site of frequent exhibitions and painting classes.

The establishment was described by *The Washington Post* in 1919 as "something like a Greenwich Village coffee house" that had "gaudy pictures created by futurists and impressionists." Its name came from a popular comic strip at the time titled Krazy Kat, whose main character was copied for use on both the front door and on shirts worn by the waiters. The strip was the genius of artist George Herriman, who created a stir at the time

because he stated that Krazy Kat was androgynous: sometimes Krazy was a male, and sometimes a female. The cartoon strip ran in major newspapers throughout the country, and featured two protagonists: Krazy Kat and Ignatz, a mouse.

The androgynous namesake of the club seems to have been a green light for early gay people in Washington, D.C., to rendezvous and meet with like individuals without exposure. The Krazy Kat club was mentioned in the published diary of Jeb Alexander called *Jeb & Dash*, written by a gay man living in 1920s D.C. He wrote that the club was a "Bohemian joint in an old stable up near Thomas Circle ... (where) artists, musicians, atheists, professors gathered."

Despite Prohibition, the club offered liquor to its patrons, and was raided several times during its existence from about 1918 to about 1925. The Sheppard Act introduced prohibition of intoxicating liquors in Washington, D.C., effective on November 1, 1917, a full two years before a national prohibition. Both were repealed in 1933.

One raid in February of 1919 was initiated when a police officer heard a gunshot coming from the

club at 1 a.m. *The Washington Post* reported that the raid resulted in "25 prisoners, including three women — self-styled artists, poets and actors, and some who worked for the government by day and masqueraded as Bohemians by night." Most of those arrested faced charges of drinking in public.

The club was run by Cleon "Throck" Throckmorton. He had been born in Atlantic City in 1897, and studied engineering at Carnegie Tech and at George Washington University before embarking on a career as a landscape and figure painter. He also worked in the theater, where he assisted on the designs for *The Emperor Jones* (1920), and later created the sets for many Eugene O'Neill's plays.

The Krazy Kat was dismantled about 1925. While the building is no longer there, having been replaced by an industrial building, several artifacts from the club do remain. Throckmorton's lusty dancing girl sketches are now displayed at *Volare*, located in Greenwich Village at 147 West Fourth Street in New York City.

ABOVE The somewhat hidden entrance to the club was off an alley, with a small sign that read "Syne of ye Krazy Kat."

LEFT A waiter dressed in Krazy Kat cartoon shirt climbs the tree house ladder to deliver drinks.

OPPOSITE PAGE Patrons enjoying a cocktail in the tree house, and owner Cleon "Throck" Throckmorton at work creating a painting at his easel.

BELOW Bohemians pose in the tree house, no doubt the best spot in the outside club.

EBBITT HOUSE, WASHINGTON, D.C.

Ebbitt House Hotel **RAZED 1926**

While many residents and tourists alike are familiar with the famed Willard Hotel on Pennsylvania Avenue, few might know that members of the Willard family operated other hotels in the city, including the Ebbitt House Hotel. It was created by combining four very large Federal style houses on the southeast corner of F and 14th Streets in 1856.

The person behind that project was William E. Ebbitt, the hotel's namesake. One of four Vermont natives and brothers, Willard was the first sibling to enter the hotel business. He renovated and expanded the Ebbitt, and kept the well-established name. He operated the popular hotel through the Civil War, until he sold it to Caleb B. Willard in 1864.

In 1872, Willard razed the original four houses comprising the hotel, and replaced them with a modern building featuring a French Mansard roof. The six-story, brick structure kept the original name of Ebbitt House. It extended down 14th Street to the adjacent house of his brother, Henry A. Willard, the proprietor of the Willard Hotel on Pennsylvania Avenue.

Ebbitt House was described by historian James Goode as featuring 25-foot coved ceilings in the lobby supported by four massive Corinthian columns. The impressive front desk was built of carved walnut, topped with marble. Its elaborately paneled bar was later reinstalled in a building at 1427 F Street, NW, in a restaurant called the Old Ebbitt Grill. The Ebbitt House was renovated in a massive scale on the exterior in 1895, when a more fanciful French Mansard roof was added to the top of the building, with wrought-iron cresting.

Patrons at the Ebbitt House Hotel included leading figures of the day, who often took rooms for years. William McKinley was one such individual, who stayed at the Ebbitt throughout his Congressional career until being elected the 25th President of the United States in 1897.

Then as now, older hotels failed to meet the new demands of its customers, and the building was razed in 1926. It was replaced by the National Press Building.

OPPOSITE PAGE *This corner view shows the scale of the original Ebbitt House Hotel at F and 14th Streets, NW.*

RIGHT *Residents and tourists take to the streets in front of the Ebbitt House Hotel during one of the city's snowstorms.*

BELOW *Old postcards show the colored clay tile roof of the Ebbitt House Hotel, and its charming café.*

Washington Hospital for Foundlings RAZED 1929

The Washington Hospital for Foundlings was located on 15th Street just south of S Street, NW. An early D.C. landowner named Joshua Pierce included the vacant lot in his will, dated April 11, 1869, "to be utilized for some sort of institution in the future." The Washington Hospital for Foundlings was incorporated the following year, but took 15 years to raise funds and construct a home on the site. They were issued a building permit on March 16, 1885.

The building was designed by architect Robert I. Fleming and built at a total cost of $23,500. Subsequent permits were granted for a variety of building extensions to the hospital and grounds. In 1896, the Washington Hospital for Foundlings had 30 children in residence, admitted 69 new children, and discharged 17 by adoption. Remarkably, the number of children that died in the hospital that year was 54.

An article in the July 2, 1898 edition of *The Washington Post* entitled "30 Crying Babies" described a complaint by neighbor Edward Dunkerly to the Commissioners of the city over his family's lack of sleep. His letter describes the nightly "suffering" inflicted on his family by the noisy orphans. It is perhaps in response to such neighbors' complaints that Architect Adolf Cluss designed a summer house for the institution in Bethesda, Maryland, which was built between 1899 and 1900.

The 1900 census reveals that 62-year-old Miss R.B. Kate was the official Matron of the Home, who oversaw 16 workers including nine nurses, one boarder, a janitor, two laundresses, a waitress, a cook, and 34 "inmates," or infants. All of the babies had been born since 1898, and several had no names, being listed as "unknown" as to the whereabouts or identity of their birthplace or their parents.

The Washington Home for Foundlings decided to move its operation in 1927 to 42nd Street and Brandywine Streets, NW, and St. Augustine's Catholic Church demolished the structure in March of 1929 to make way for a proposed school, convent, and large church building.

The convent and school were built by 1929, but the onset of the Great Depression halted work on the large cathedral at the foundation level. There it

stood, covered and used as a one-story sanctuary for decades until it was finally built upon and converted into the Bishop's Gate condominium complex in 1980.

ABOVE *The Washington Hospital for Foundlings at 1715 15th Street NW. The site today is home to the Bishop's Gate condominium complex.*

OPPOSITE PAGE AND RIGHT *Young orphans are entertained in their playroom circa 1921 by one of their major benefactors, Lt. George Pickett III.*

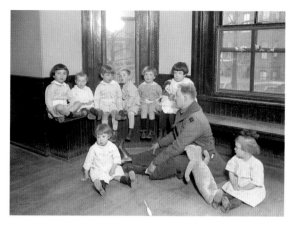

Alexander Graham Bell Mansion RAZED 1930

Noted American telephone inventor Alexander Graham Bell (1847–1922) built his house at 1331 Connecticut Avenue, NW beginning in June of 1891 at an impressive cost of $31,000. Like many inventors, he integrated new technology and experiments into the design, including what was one of the earliest experiments in household air conditioning.

Bell had been born in Scotland, but emigrated along with his parents to Canada in 1870, when he had already been working as a teacher to deaf mutes through his 1864 "invisible speech" method. Several years later, young Bell began to teach at Boston University, where he met his future wife, Mabel Hubbard. She had become deaf due to scarlet fever, and was the daughter of wealthy lawyer Gardiner Green Hubbard (1822–97).

Following his daughter's marriage, in 1877 Hubbard became Bell's business manager and the first President of the Bell Telephone Company. Alexander and Mabel first moved into a newly purchased house at 1500 Rhode Island Avenue, NW just a year after he had become internationally famous for demonstrating the telephone in public at the Philadelphia Centennial Exhibition. The first words spoken by telephone were "Watson, come here, I want you," which Bell uttered to his lab assistant Thomas Watson in an adjoining room. After 1500 Rhode Island Avenue was damaged by fire they sold it to Vice President Levi P. Morton, and then began construction of 1331 Connecticut Avenue.

Bell established the Volta Bureau in Georgetown in 1880, where much of his inventing and experiments were undertaken. He had architects Hornblower and Marshall design a wing on the Connecticut Avenue house for his famous "Wednesday Evenings" that entertained scientists and society for decades.

At the house, Bell also experimented with an early form of air conditioning: on a hot summer day, he placed a block of ice in the attic covered with salt, to which he connected a large diameter tube extending to his office. His invention managed to reduce the temperature of the room from 90 to 65 degrees.

The house was also designed with a large rear yard that led to the two houses of his daughters, facing 18th Street. After his death, the house was inherited by his daughter, Mrs. Gilbert Grosvenor, who ran it as an antique shop and tea room. It was razed in 1930 to make way for an office building.

ABOVE *Hornblower and Marshall designed the mansion at 1331 Connecticut Avenue. It originally had a south-facing garden that was later replaced.*

OPPOSITE PAGE *Bell Mansion, photographed after the south salon had replaced the garden.*

ALEXANDER GRAHAM BELL

With his telephone a financial success, Alexander Graham Bell set his sights on other innovative inventions. He constructed an electromagnetic device to help locate the bullet lodged in President Garfield following his assassination attempt (see page 38). What garners little attention today are Bell's contributions to flight, beginning in the 1890s with propeller and kite-flying experiments. In 1909, his *Silver Dart* made the first successful powered flight in Canada. Bell spent the last decade of his life improving hydrofoil designs, and in 1919 he built a hydrofoil that set a world water-speed record that was not broken until 1963.

Albaugh's Opera House RAZED 1930

Few might have envisioned designing a building that would serve both military and opera simultaneously, but that was exactly the purpose of Albaugh's Opera House, constructed at 15th and E Streets, NW. The building was constructed by the Washington Light Infantry, who utilized the ground floor as a drill hall. The upper stories were designed for large opera productions, and as a source of rent for the Infantry.

Established in 1836, the Washington Light Infantry had served in every conflict since the Mexican War. The Infantry was later incorporated into the District of Columbia National Guard.

Albaugh's Opera House was designed by architects W. Bruce Gray and J. L. Smithmeyer, who practiced in Washington from 1878 to 1885. The *Washington Star* described the interior on opening night, November 10, 1884, which featured Rossini's masterpiece *Semiramide*. It noted that the auditorium measured 75 by 90 feet, with a stage measuring 90 by 51 feet, allowing the largest of opera productions to be staged. It was lit with electric lights, a novelty for the era, and featured an elaborate coffered ceiling. President Chester A. Arthur attending opening night.

The opera building was named after its Opera manager, John W. Albaugh, who was also frequently found on stage himself.

Albaugh was born in Baltimore, Maryland on September 30, 1837, and was married in 1866 to actress Mary Lomax Mitchell, sister of the more famous actress Maggie Mitchell. He was attracted early to the stage. On November 24, 1853 when just 16 years old he took the female part of Portia in the *Merchant of Venice* at a performance in Baltimore.

Albaugh continued to perform throughout his tenure as manager in various leading roles. His last appearance on the Albaugh stage was as Macbeth with Helen Modjeska about 1894. He then built and owned the Lyceum Theatre in Baltimore.

The building also housed important conventions, such as the International Council on Women in 1888, presided over by Susan B. Anthony. A constitution was drafted, and the group established national meetings every three years and international meetings every five years. Contrary to what may have been perceived about this pioneering group, the ICW did not actively promote women's suffrage as it did not want to upset its more conservative members.

Albaugh's Opera House was remodeled and renamed twice; once in 1901 as the Chase Opera House and once in 1913 as Poli's Theater.

The planning of the Federal Triangle in 1928 called for Albaugh's Opera House to be torn down, and the building was razed two years later, in 1930.

INTERNATIONAL COUNCIL OF WOMEN

In March and April of 1888, Albaugh's Opera House was the site of the founding convention of the International Council of Women (ICW), the first women's organization to work across national boundaries advocating human rights for women. Women leaders from professional organizations, trade unions, arts groups and benevolent societies came to meet with 80 speakers and 49 delegates representing 53 women's organizations from nine countries. Woman's rights pioneers Rachel Foster Avery and Susan B. Anthony (above) were responsible for organizing much of the first ICW. Today the ICW is composed of representatives from 70 countries and has its headquarters in Lasaunne, Switzerland.

ABOVE RIGHT *Susan B. Anthony, who attended and led the International Council of Women conference held at Albaugh's Opera House in 1888.*

LEFT *Captain Richard France, depicted in 1841, an early leader of the Washington Light Infantry.*

OPPOSITE PAGE *Albaugh's Opera House, with the drill hall for the Washington Light Infantry on the ground floor.*

RICHARD FRANCE.

Center Market RAZED 1931

For 60 years, virtually all of Washington shopped at the Center Market on Pennsylvania Avenue, NW. It was considered a model modern market when it opened in 1871. Designed by Adolph Cluss, its location between Seventh and Ninth Streets at the junction of four streetcar routes, virtually guaranteed success.

The brick building was an impressive 300 feet long, and cost $500,000 to construct. It operated six days a week, from the early dawn hours to noon. Adjacent to the building on Constitution Avenue was an area for an additional 300 farmers' wagons selling all varieties of homegrown goods. They traveled up and down Seventh Street, NW, which was lined with orchards just beyond the city boundaries.

The market had replaced a rather unsightly market that had grown unsanitary since its founding at the site in 1800. Known as the "Marsh Market" because of the low soft ground on which it was built, it had been designed by James Hoban and Clotworth Stevens. Fish vendors were known to keep live fish in baskets lowered into the stagnant Washington City Canal at the edge of the building along what was then B Street (see Washington City Canal, page 16).

Center Market was expanded in the 1880s and grew to house 1,000 vendors inside. Many local shops had a branch of their business in the market, selling bread, meat, poultry, pastries, flowers, fish, and more. It featured the city's first cold storage area, and had its own artesian well and an ice plant.

Vintage photographs reveal that toward the end of its existence, the market housed a "coliseum" that at one point offered ice skating. The private corporation operating the market was plagued with charges of running a monopoly, and it was abolished by Congress in 1922. The Department of Agriculture ran the market for a few years until the building was torn down and replaced with the National Archives building in 1931.

WASHINGTON'S MARKETS

Today, only one original market remains in Washington where a resident might find fresh pork. Eastern Market on Capitol Hill retains a popular and lively old-fashioned market atmosphere, although it recently required a complete renovation after a brush with a fire. Two market buildings remain; the Georgetown Market at M and Potomac Streets, NW is operated as a gourmet grocery store, and the O Street Market at Seventh and O Streets, NW is undergoing a transformation into a modern grocery store. Long gone are the Western Market at 21st and K Streets, NW, the new Center Market at Fifth and K Streets, NW (which replaced the Northern Liberties Market), and the Municipal Fish Market (above) at 11th and Water Streets, SW.

ABOVE *The Municipal Fish Market at 11th and Water Streets, SW.*

LEFT *A circa-1920 photograph of the Old Dutch Market. Although the market is long gone, the building that housed it on the corner of 20th and P Streets, NW remains.*

RIGHT *The north facade of Center Market, facing Pennsylvania Avenue, just one half of the massive, U-shaped building.*

The Old Brick Capitol **RAZED 1932**

It is perhaps fitting that the U.S. Supreme Court Building sits at the very spot where a Civil War-era prison was once located, housing political enemies and Confederate spies with no regard for a fair trial. The bulky brick building, whose foundations dated back to 1815, had been used as a private school and a boarding house for Congressmen for decades, and was purchased by the federal government in 1861. Its windows were secured with heavy wooden slats, and the building was quickly converted into a prison.

Armed militia outside the building and its extensive wooden rear addition prevented escapes, and more importantly, contact or the passing of weapons from the many southern sympathizers living in Washington at the time. Prisoners included the mayor of Washington, James G. Berret, arrested for speaking against the federal government. He and other male prisoners were eventually sent to prisons in New York and elsewhere. In the rear courtyard, the only person ever executed for war crimes, Andersonville Prison Superintendent Henry Wirz, was hanged on November 10, 1865.

The prison also held female prisoners, including Confederate spy Mrs. Rose O'Neal Greenhow and her young daughter. She had been arrested for passing along information on military movements and fortification building to the southern armies. Female prisoners were eventually loaded onto steamships and delivered to the South where they were to remain for the duration of the Civil War.

After its use as a prison, the building was sold in 1865 for $20,000. It was converted into three massive Second Empire houses by sergeant-at-arms of the Senate George T. Brown. Several decades later, they were used as the headquarters of the National Women's Party. The houses and others on the block were razed in 1932 for the construction of the U.S. Supreme Court Building.

OPPOSITE PAGE *During the Civil War, wooden boards over the windows prevented prisoners from escaping.*

RIGHT *Confederate spy Rose O'Neal Greenhow and her young daughter.*

BELOW *The Lincoln conspirators were hanged in the courtyard of the Washington Penitentiary in July, 1865.*

CONGRESSIONAL STALEMATE

The Old Brick Capitol building was built by 38 local citizens that feared Congress would relocate the Capitol city following the burning by the British in August of 1814. They completed the $25,000 structure and it was the only available meeting space for Congress in the city when their term began in December of 1815. The Senate met on the first floor, and the House of Representatives on the second. Because the two houses could not agree on which floor the inauguration of President James Monroe would take place, they broke the stalemate by being sworn in outside the building, establishing a tradition of an outside inaugural that has lasted to this day.

Wisconsin Avenue Reservoir REMOVED 1932

If you were to visit the historic files kept at the Peabody Room in the Georgetown branch of the D.C. Public Library to research the Wisconsin Avenue Reservoir, you might be surprised to discover that it was once located right under the library building itself. It was removed in 1932 for the construction of the Colonial Revival library building after being abandoned and unused since 1897.

The reservoir was an engineering feat, and an important element of the city's early and innovative Washington Aqueduct system. By 1850, the water supply for the city was woefully inadequate, and Congress had voted to have the Army Corps of Engineers study the problem and provide a solution. After exploring a way to bring water from the upper reaches of Rock Creek was deemed unreliable, a second plan designed by Lt. Montgomery C. Meigs in 1852 was agreed.

It was an ambitious plan, and a costly one. It would involve the laying of 12 miles of pipes from Great Falls, Maryland, where a small dam was constructed. The nine-foot diameter pipes would lead the water by gravity to the first of three reservoirs in the city. The first of these was a receiving reservoir located at the city's western boundary, now known as the Dalecarlia. It stored and removed sediment from the water. It was connected to pipes leading to a second distributing reservoir located on Conduit Road, known as the Georgetown Reservoir today. The road, now known as known as MacArthur Boulevard, was created for the construction of the aqueduct system itself, and to cover the pipes. A third reservoir was built at the corner of Wisconsin Avenue and R Streets, NW. Pumps brought water up Wisconsin Avenue to the reservoir, and its location at the top of the hill meant that significant water pressure was available to all of Georgetown.

The Georgetown reservoir was a complex, brick dome, lined with plaster. It stood an impressive five stories tall and was 120 feet in diameter. On completion, the Army Corps of Engineers hired architect Paul J. Peltz to design a cast-iron cap for the structure. It featured a trident and dolphin motif built into each of the six-foot tall sculptures atop the building. The aqueduct system cost $3.5 million and took 2,000 laborers 14 years to build.

OPPOSITE PAGE *The Wisconsin Avenue Reservoir, with only the retaining wall and a few other clues still located where the Georgetown Public Library stands today.*

BELOW *The unprecedented size of the water pipes became an attraction in themselves before they were installed.*

Harvey's Original Restaurant **RAZED 1932**

Harvey's Restaurant was perhaps the best known eating establishment in Washington, D.C., and also the center of power and networking for much of its more than 150 years in business. Originally named Harvey's Ladies' and Gentlemen's Oyster Saloon, it was established by brothers George W. and Thomas M. Harvey in 1858 at the corner of 11th and C Streets, NW. With the huge influx of residents and business owners in Washington during the Civil War, the brothers began to experiment with various ways of cooking oysters, eventually perfecting the steam cooking method.

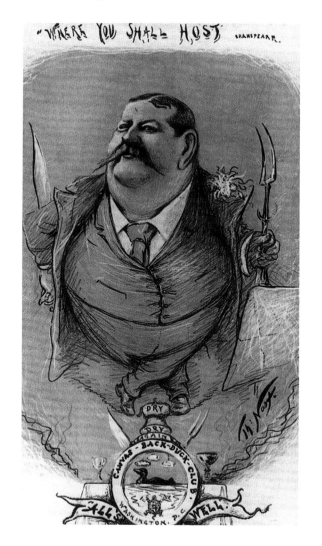

The restaurant's first location was a converted blacksmith shop, with additions built as the business thrived. The newly found delicacy was extremely popular, and by 1863 the restaurant was steaming an impressive 500 wagonloads of oysters each and every week. Piles of oyster shells as high as 50 feet were described surrounding the restaurant.

Harvey's changed locations in 1866, when it moved to a newly renovated, cast-iron facade building located at 11th Street and Pennsylvania Avenue, NW. There, they entertained political and literary leaders for more than 65 years. Every President from Ulysses S. Grant to Franklin D. Roosevelt dined in the building. In 1932 it moved to a building adjacent to the Mayflower Hotel on Connecticut Avenue and DeSales Street, NW and the cast-iron building was razed that same year to create the Federal Triangle project.

One regular at the restaurant was famous New York cartoonist Thomas Nast (1840–1902). He drew a caricature of founder George Harvey that was used in their advertising for decades. He and others invented clubs with the sole intention of meeting monthly to dine at the restaurant, using eccentric names like the Canvas Back Duck Club and the Tapeworm Club.

In 1970, the establishment moved to 18th and K Streets, NW when the Farragut North Metro station was built on the location of its Connecticut Avenue building. Shortly thereafter, the restaurant moved to the suburbs where it remains today.

ABOVE *Harvey's was located for 66 years in this 1866 cast-iron building just east of the Old Post Office Building on Pennsylvania Avenue.*

LEFT *Thomas Nast's plump caricature of George W. Harvey was used in the restaurant's advertising.*

OPPOSITE PAGE *Harvey's Restaurant was frequently patronized by performers at the "Palace of Burlesque" (the New Lyceum Theatre) next door.*

Original Calvert Street Bridge

MOVED 1934, DISMANTLED 1935

The deep Rock Creek Park posed a serious obstacle for Washington development north of the city. Travelers headed north had to drive horses and early cars down the steep embankment, cross the shallow water, and climb up the other side.

A temporary wooden bridge was eventually built over the water in the 1870s, leading from the Adams Morgan neighborhood to the emerging summer estates in what is today Woodley Park. The Engineer Commissioner reported no immediate plans for constructing a permanent bridge in 1887, citing the rugged topography as not worth tackling.

Senator Francis G. Newlands and his business, the Chevy Chase Land Company, had purchased enormous amounts of land from the termination of Connecticut Avenue all the way to Chevy Chase in secret negotiations to keep prices down. His Rock Creek Railway Company was formed to transport new home buyers to the north of the city, and it required adequate bridges to span Rock Creek.

Construction commenced on a large iron truss bridge leading from Columbia Road to Connecticut Avenue in Woodley Park that was completed in 1891. It was built by the Edgemore Bridge Company. When completed, the ownership of the bridge was turned over to the city government.

The original Calvert Street Bridge was an impressive site. It was 755 feet long, and cost an estimated $70,000. The wrought iron used for its construction weighed a total of 1,266 tons. Beginning in 1917, however, District Commissioners hired local architect George Oakley Totten, Jr., to design a new Calvert Street bridge. The Commission of Fine Arts (CFA) determined that the resulting design was too costly and ornate, and feared that it might overshadow the newly completed Connecticut Avenue Bridge to the west. The design was discarded, and the CFA selected Paul Philippe Cret as chief designer for a new bridge. His first design was also rejected, and the CFA finally settled on a masonry design with multiple arches.

The need for crossing Rock Creek remained during the construction period of the new bridge, however, which was begun in 1934. The decision was made to move the original iron bridge 80 feet downstream to be used for diverted traffic until the new bridge was completed the following year.

In the early dawn hours of June 7, 1934, the five 130 foot piers of the bridge were lowered onto a specially made track of horizontal girders, and outfitted with wheels. At 5 a.m., workers cut the railroad tracks on the bridge above, and a series of block and tackle was attached to the bridge with a windlass. Horses took over, and incredibly in just seven hours and 15 minutes, the bridge was at its new position 80 feet to the west.

Thousands of onlookers had gathered to watch the unusual feat, and after it was in place, the railroad track was reattached and open for traffic in less than two hours. Following the completion of the masonry arch in 1935, the original Calvert Street Bridge was dismantled for scrap.

RIGHT *The original Calvert Street Bridge, which was moved 80 feet downstream in 1934 for the construction of its replacement.*

BELOW *After years of design review and delays, the new Calvert Street Bridge, seen in the foreground, opened in 1935. It was renamed Duke Ellington Bridge in 1974.*

Washington Riding Academy RAZED 1936

For nearly 50 years, the Washington Riding Academy stood on the south side of the 2200 block of P Street at the foot of the P Street Bridge, offering easy access to Rock Creek Park for many horse enthusiasts. Built in 1887, the massive building housed stables, a riding ring, and hay loft.

Architect George S. Cooper provided the plans for the building, which measured 100 by 130 feet and cost an estimated $20,000 to build. Construction started in June of 1887. The owner on the building permit was listed as a J. D. Brown, and the builder of the structure was listed as Chaz Federline.

The stable was located in the basement, and the enormous riding ring was at street level, open to the clerestory windows on the second floor. Horses entered from P Street through a vast arch, with a club office located through the arch on 21st Street. The second floor offered club rooms, a kitchen reception rooms, and bathing rooms.

The Academy opened in 1888, boasting a stock of 20 well-trained, thoroughbred saddle horses, with space for boarding an additional 130 horses for owners residing nearby. The building also contained 13,000 square feet for the storage of carriages.

Classes lasting six months in duration included those for tandem riding and driving, and four-in-hand driving for men and women. Couples could also be instructed in "music riding," added by whistles and music orchestrated to change tempos and the stride of horses.

Early prominent members included President Cleveland and his cabinet, and in 1916, Mr. and Mrs. Ambrose Preece, natives of England, were lured to the club from New York City to take over horsemanship. They eventually started their own riding club called the Preece Riding School near Massachusetts Avenue and 30th Street.

Like many other riding clubs in the city, the Washington Riding Academy closed its doors during the Great Depression of the 1930s. It was demolished in 1936 to make way for a Gulf Oil gas and service station that is known today as the Embassy Service Station. The southern portion of the facility was replaced by an office building that was later converted into apartments.

ABOVE *A City Directory advertisement for the Academy.*

LEFT *Mrs. Ambrose Preece and her husband came from New York to manage the Washington Riding Academy.*

OPPOSITE PAGE *The Riding Academy building on the southwest corner of 21st and P Streets, NW.*

McLean Mansion RAZED 1939

With a fifth major expansion in 1907, the John R. McLean mansion at 1500 Eye Street became the city's largest house, taking up the entire block. Originally built in 1860, all earlier versions of the exterior facade were incorporated into the 1907 redesign by noted architect John Russell Pope.

John R. McLean had begun renting the house on the site in 1884. He purchased it a short time later, and had it enlarged in 1886, 1894, and 1896 before the major transformation took place in 1907.

McLean had inherited a fortune when his father Washington McLean (a manufacturer of steamboats on the Ohio River) died in 1890. John McLean married wealthy Emily Beale, the daughter of General Edward F. Beale and purchased *The Washington Post* in 1905 (see page 89). They had the house redesigned for entertaining on a massive scale. The first floor ceiling height was an impressive 30 feet, and the grand staircase featured a balcony overlooking McPherson Square. The household was tended to by 30 servants that lived on the third floor. The entertaining rooms included a massive entrance hall, dining room with three long tables, library, conservatory, and three reception rooms lined with priceless tapestries and artwork.

The interiors of the mansion were designed by noted New York interior designer to the wealthy, Elsie De Wolf. John Russell Pope had designed many of the architectural elements and lighting fixtures to resemble or copy their counterparts found in European castles and palaces. To escape Washington's hot summers, the McLeans also had an estate named Friendship built on upper Wisconsin Avenue set on 60 acres and valued at $7 million.

John and Emily McLean had one child together, Edward B. McLean, and he would marry heiress Evalyn Walsh, the only daughter of spectacularly wealthy Senator and Mrs. Thomas F. Walsh. Senator Walsh had made his fortune as owner of the Camp Bird Gold Mine in Colorado.

Evalyn Walsh McLean recalled in her autobiography *Father Struck it Rich* that one party held in the McLean mansion just before World War I for George Bakhmeteff, the Russian Ambassador to the United States, was attended by just 48 guests, but cost $40,000. The dining room had been filled with flowers imported from London.

The house was inherited by Edward and Evalyn McLean upon the death of John McLean in 1916. The couple demonstrated their enormous wealth by purchasing the famed Hope Diamond. It was frequently placed on Evalyn's Boston Terrier to the amusement of her dinner guests. They ultimately spent $100 million on travel and entertaining.

Evalyn Walsh McLean rented the mansion to the federal government in 1935 to house the Federal Emergency Relief Agency, the Works Progress Administration, and the National Bituminous Coal Commission. It was sold in 1939, and razed to make way for the Lafayette office building. Mrs McLean moved into a house in Georgetown where she died in 1945.

ABOVE *A circa-1909 photograph of Mrs. John R. McLean taken in the long gallery.*

LEFT *Statuary and Ionic columns adorned the conservatory.*

OPPOSITE PAGE *Resembling more an art gallery than a private residence, the McLean mansion covered an entire city block.*

General Noble Redwood Tree House

PLACED IN STORAGE 1932, BURNED 1940

The western world first became aware of giant sequoia trees in 1848. The appropriately named John Wood made the discovery when he settled in California just before the gold rush. The trees eventually created a sensation, and were soon harvested for their precious wood.

A tradition of naming the giant sequoias after famous Americans began in the 1860s. One such tree was named after Brigadier General John Willock Noble (1831–1912), who had spearheaded a law in 1891 to preserve millions of acres of government-owned forests in the Western states. That expanded the protection of two patches of sequoia redwoods the year prior called the General Grant National Park and Sequoia National Park in California, signed into law by President Harrison.

Twenty-three lumbermen had taken a week to cut down the General Noble Tree which was located in the General Grant National Park in Tulare, California. The 300-foot-tall tree had a 26-foot diameter and was a remarkable 85 feet in circumference. It was estimated to have been 2,000 years old. The resulting stump stood 50 feet tall, and was sliced into 30 sections and carefully numbered for transportation on the railroad. The trunk had been hollowed out to create a tree house that incorporated a circular stair in its center. It was reassembled for exhibition at the 1893 World's Columbian Exposition in Chicago, Illinois. The novelty made an otherwise grim government exhibit a sensation.

Following the fair, the tree was moved to Washington, D.C., and installed on a plot of ground on the National Mall near the old Agriculture Building. When the Mall was redesigned in 1932, the tree was dissembled and stored in large pieces at the Department of Agriculture experimental farm in Arlington, Virginia. The farm was slated to become part of the site of the massive Pentagon complex, and it is thought that the tree was burned as scrap wood in 1940.

RIGHT *Lumbermen took a full week to cut the base from the 300-foot-tall sequoia in General Grant National Park.*

OPPOSITE PAGE *The Noble Tree House was a popular tourist attraction on the National Mall from 1894 to 1930.*

Copyright 1892 By C.C. Curtis

Washington-Hoover Airport **RAZED 1941**

One might certainly expect the life of an airport with 114 daily arrivals and departures to last more than 11 years, but that was not the case with the Washington-Hoover Airport located just across Potomac River and the 14th Street Bridge in Arlington, Virginia.

The airport was one of the first in the country, and had formed in 1930 by joining two smaller airports that had coexisted side by side and been built just a few years earlier. Hoover Field had begun flying mail and passengers to Philadelphia on July 16, 1926; Washington Airport began passenger flights to New York in June of 1928.

The new main terminal building of the Washington-Hoover Airport had been designed in streamlined art moderne style by the architectural firm of Holden, Stott, & Hutchinson in 1930. It featured an open lobby, waiting room, restaurant, and office space for the owners of the airport, the Washington Air Terminals Corporation. A central glass-fronted tower was designed with curved glass windows to accommodate the newly created career of air-traffic controllers. They guided planes to the runways at night using green and red flood lights.

The origin of Hoover Field—named after then Secretary of Commerce and future President Herbert Hoover—was wealthy Philadelphia resident Thomas E. Mitten who had won a contract in 1926 from the U.S. Postal system to transport airmail between the two cities. He had purchased three 10-passenger planes from Dutch inventor Anthony H. G. Fokker's factory in New Jersey.

After failing to secure permission to use the military Bolling Field airstrip south of Washington, Mitten purchased a 37-acre pasture at this site and built an airstrip in 1926, which became Hoover Field. Pilot Henry Berliner leased an adjoining parcel (which became Washington Airport) and began regularly scheduled passenger flights to New York.

The combined 1930 airport facility grew fast, soon with 70 scheduled flights a day, operated by Luddington Airlines (later bought by Eastern Airlines).

The airport's location was somewhat cursed, however, as industrial sites and commercial buildings close by prevented expansion. After 12 years of Congressional delays, funds were provided in 1941 for a new airport a few miles south on the Potomac, which grew into today's Ronald Reagan Washington International Airport.

Eleven years after it opened, Washington-Hoover Airport was razed to make way for the massive Pentagon complex.

ABOVE *The passenger terminal at Hoover Airport was used for 11 years, from 1930 until 1941.*

LEFT *The airport's rather crude tarmac and landing strips nonetheless supported hourly flights to New York City.*

RIGHT *An aerial photograph of Washington-Hoover Airport from 1932, showing the bridge that was later replaced with the 14th Street Bridge, leading to the city. A private club and swimming pool complex can be seen on the left.*

The Arcade RAZED 1948

The Arcade was an immense building once located at 14th Street and Park Road, NW in the Columbia Heights neighborhood. It was a familiar landmark for city residents headed to everything from a beauty pageant to a wrestling match that was held in the cavernous entertainment complex. The building itself was an early example of adaptive reuse, having been built as a car barn for the Georgetown Railroad Company circa 1892. In 1909, a new car barn was constructed two miles further north to serve an expanding city, and the 300 by 142 feet Arcade building was sold to the Arcadia Market and Amusement Company.

The Arcade opened for business on February 14, 1910, with 10,000 residents attending the festivities. It was located at 3134 to 3138 14th Street, diagonally across from the Tivoli Theater. The reuse of the former car barn lent itself to a wide variety of uses. The building boasted a movie theater that seated 300 patrons, in addition to 14 bowling alleys, pool and billiard halls, skating rink, basketball courts, card rooms, lounges, a market, running track, tennis courts, and an enclosed dancing pavilion on the roof. An advertisement in 1910 indicated that the theater would only show "high class, clean pictures for intelligent people."

Admission to the building itself cost 15 cents for adults and 10 cents for children between the hours of 3 and 6 p.m. Prices in the evening hours were raised to 25 and 15 cents respectively.

The building featured an alluring array of amusements and attractions, including the Mysterious Japanese and Crystal Maze, the Down and Outside, the Soup Bowl, the Cave of the Winds, and the Human Roulette Wheel, which could twirl as many as 50 patrons at a time. Ultimately, entire fairs and exhibitions were held within the enclosed facility. The building was advertised as "Washington's Madison Square Garden" in the 1925 *Book of Washington* published by the Washington Board of Trade.

The Arcade was reviewed in the magazine *Moving Picture* in 1910 by an anonymous reader that wrote "it is jammed every night, all the evening, in spite of the fact that one must enter the building, walk up stairs and down a long hall … you will find one new and two old releases nightly, three full reels for a nickel." The building's large ballroom opened on March 12, 1910, in which formal hops were held on Wednesday evenings for a charge of 50 cents per couple. It was also the venue for dance classes, fashion shows, formal dances, ceremonials, lectures, and private parties.

The building's picture garden was remodeled for the summer of 1913. In January of 1919 the entire complex was remodeled, with a third floor space configured into a dance hall; the space had been utilized as a practice facility for the World War I Army Signal Corps.

In November of 1925, the Arcade became home to the newly organized American Basketball Association's "Palace Five" team. A crowd of 2,500 fans watched the inaugural game against the Brooklyn Five, whom they beat 18 to 17.

By 1929 the building was being marketed as the Arcadia, home to the Arcadia Sporting Club, Arcadia Market, Bowling, Billiards, Dancing Classes, a Card Party Room and a Ballroom. Like many early amusement facilities, the Great Depression ultimately led to its demise.

The Arcade was razed in 1948. Today the site is occupied by a $150 million retail development known as the DC USA complex, which opened in March 2008.

THE ARCADIA

14th and Park Road N.W.

Washington's Madison Square Garden

This Beautiful Building Houses—	The Auditorium in Which Can Be Held—
Arcadia Sporting Club	Boxing Exhibitions
Beautiful Lounge	Fashion Shows
Arcadia Market	Basketball
Auditorium	Track Meets
Rest Rooms	Tennis
Bowling	Fairs
Billiards	Dances
Dancing Classes	Lectures
Pocket Billiards	Ceremonials
Small Ball Room	Exhibitions
Card Party Room	Wrestling Matches

Officers

JOHN S. BLICK
President and Gen. Mgr.
HON. WM. A. RODENBERG
First Vice President
EUGENE S. COCHRAN
Second Vice President
C. CHESTER CAYWOOD
Secretary
HARRY M. CRANDALL
Treasurer

ARCADIA

MARKET & AMUSEMENT CO.
INCORPORATED

14TH STREET AND PARK ROAD

PHONES: COL. 9800, 9801, 9802, 9803

Directors

HON. WM. A. RODENBERG
Chairman
JOHN S. BLICK
C. CHESTER CAYWOOD
EUGENE S. COCHRAN
HARRY M. CRANDALL
G. W. FORSBERG
M. G. GIBBS
J. SHULMAN

ABOVE *The Arcade became known as the Arcadia by the time of this 1925 advertisement.*

LEFT *The Arcade featured a movie theater, bowling alleys, a skating rink, and tennis courts.*

OPPOSITE PAGE *The Arcade opened on Valentine's Day, 1910 with 10,000 local residents joining the festivities.*

Francis Scott Key Mansion RAZED 1948

The house that Francis Scott Key (1779–1843) purchased in 1805 on M Street in Georgetown near 35th Street, NW had been built a few years earlier by Thomas Clark. Key and his wife, the former Mary Taylor Lloyd, would reside in what would become Key Mansion for more than 20 years.

Key was a native of Frederick, Maryland, and had attended law school at St. John's College. He moved to Georgetown to become a partner in his uncle's law firm. In the rather humble Federal-styled house, Key and his wife would raise a family of six children. Key built a one-story addition to the house on the west side to serve as his law office. He also created a rear garden with growing plants that spelled out each of his children's names.

A religious man, Key considered leaving the legal profession to become a minister for his church, Saint John's Episcopal Church in Georgetown. He also served in the Georgetown Light Infantry in June of 1814, when the city was under siege from the British during the War of 1812.

Key came to the defense of a Dr. William Beanes who had inflated a story about three British officers disturbing the peace. Beanes was captured and held as a noncombatant prisoner of war on the British admiral's flagship. Key boarded the American cutter *Minden* for negotiations with the British authorities during a truce period on the Chesapeake Bay on September 7, 1814. Key succeeded in releasing Beanes and they were put aboard a small boat and ordered to stay just outside the harbor at Baltimore. The British officers would not allow them to leave for fear that they would reveal their plans of attack on Fort McHenry, which protected Baltimore.

The commandant of Fort McHenry defiantly ordered a local seamstress to create an enormous American flag, measuring 29 feet tall by 39 feet long, with 15 stars and stripes, representing each State of the Union at the time. He raised the flag in front of the looming British fleet and Key and Beanes witnessed the attack from their boat on September 12, 1814. Key began to pen his lyrics to what would become the national anthem while aboard his vessel, completing the hymn when he returned to Baltimore. As the lyrics go, the flag was still there after an all night battle that resulted in the British retreating following heavy casualties. "The Star-Spangled Banner" was eventually signed into law as the national anthem by President Herbert Hoover on March 2, 1931.

The Key Mansion was purchased by attorney Hugh T. Taggart and opened as a museum in 1907. It languished afterwards, and was purchased by the National Park Service in 1931. Plans for the Whitehurst Freeway and Key Highway called for the removal of the house. Several years of unsuccessful attempts at relocating the house failed and it was eventually razed in 1948.

THE KEY PROSECUTOR

While famous for his lyrics to the National Anthem, few might remember that Francis Scott Key was the city's district attorney for eight years. The ambitious lawyer was a staunch defender of slavery, and a case he was involved with in 1835 resulted in the city's first racial riots. As documented in *Snow Storm in August* by Jefferson Morley, the case surrounded an incident when a 19-year-old slave named Arthur Bowen entered the bedroom of his owner Anna Thorton, armed with an axe. He fled, but the story spread, and an angry mob took to the streets, especially targeting a freed black restaurateur named Beverly Snow. The twist in the case came when Thorton herself revealed that her husband may well have been the slave's father.

LEFT *The Key Mansion as a museum, shortly after its conversion in 1907. Key's one-story office on the right side was then being used as a grocery store.*

RIGHT *A portrait of Francis Scott Key.*

OPPOSITE PAGE *The Key Mansion museum featured its namesake's portrait hung over the center window. The house is shown here dressed for a patriotic occasion.*

The Wilkins Mansion **RAZED 1949**

The Washington Post has long been associated with the Meyer and Graham families, but it had earlier brought vast fortunes to the Beriah Wilkins family, who purchased the paper in 1889. They then resided in a rather modest brick townhouse at 1709 Massachusetts Avenue. In 1902, the family constructed and moved into their new stone mansion at 1711 Massachusetts Avenue. It was completed in 1902 at a cost of an astounding $110,000. Its architect was Appleton P. Clark, Jr.

The first issue of *The Post*, as it was then known, was printed on December 6, 1877. It was a modest, four-page paper that reported on local events and activities. It grew slowly, issuing a 16-page Sunday edition by the time Wilkins acquired a majority interest in January of 1889. Renamed *The Washington Post*, he instituted a new policy of a thoroughly independent paper, somewhat unusual at the time. As a result, the paper quickly grew with readership, revenue, and advertisements. Wilkins purchased the minority ownership in April of 1894. He then became the paper's editor and publisher, installing his son John as business manager and secretary, and his son Robert as the treasurer.

The *Post* scooped several other local and East Coast newspapers with news events of the day, such as the Boston Fire and Johnstown flood in 1889. It also began a long tradition of posting news bulletins outside its offices at 1337 E Street, NW during the night for those too eager to wait for the morning print edition (see Washington Post Building, page 89).

Beriah Wilkins married Emily J. Robinson on October 18, 1870 in Marysville, Ohio, and in 1883 was elected an Ohio Congressional Representative. He was well established in Washington business circles and private clubs, and led the local community in commissioning the District Municipal building on Pennsylvania Avenue. He established the Washington Board of Trade, and served for many years on the Citizens Relief Committee, which raised funds for the city's poor. He retired from Congress in 1889 to focus on *The Washington Post*.

Wilkins died on June 7, 1905, and John R. McLean purchased the *Post* in October of that year. The mansion was eventually sold by the family in the 1930s to the Fairmont School, an all-female institution that had been established in 1899.

The school offered a four-year college preparatory course, two-year junior college course, academic courses, art, music, domestic science, athletics, and "every subject that should and could be instilled into the mind of American womanhood," according to its advertisement in 1924. Pictures taken at the school in the 1940s suggest that much of the original Wilkins furniture and furnishings remained in the house.

The Wilkins Mansion was put up for sale in 1949. Along with others on the block, it was razed that same year to make way for the Boston House apartment building that was built in 1950.

RIGHT *The cover to John Phillip Sousa's composition, "The Washington Post March."*

LEFT *Beriah Wilkins, owner of* The Washington Post.

OPPOSITE PAGE *The Wilkins Mansion at 1711 Massachusetts Avenue, built at a cost of $110,000.*

THE *POST* IS MUSIC TO MY EARS

Perhaps the most surprising attribute of Wilkins' tenure at the *Post* was hiring John Philip Sousa to compose "The Washington Post March." It was written and performed in June of 1890 for the gathering of the *Post's* Amateur Author's Association on the grounds of the Smithsonian. It quickly became a favorite for municipal bands all across the nation, and over two million copies were printed and sold. Its prominence spread, and the march was introduced into the royal court by the Empress of China in 1895, and even played whenever Austrian singer Jean de Reszke's famed racing horses won a race.

Dressed Buildings CEASED 1950s

In the days when electricity and labor were both cheap and flag bunting material plentiful, like most cities and towns across America, Washington's buildings were frequently draped and dressed. The entire facade might be draped with the American flag bunting, or other colorful combinations of fabric. Long strings of electric lights were also used to create a festive atmosphere at night, attracting sightseers to buildings that have never witnessed so many lights in one place.

The reasons and the occasions varied for the dressing of a building or house. It might have meant to celebrate the 4th of July, or to commemorate an influential citizen, policeman, or firefighter during a somber funeral possession. Either way, the ritual slowly came to an end by the 1950s.

STRETCHING THE FLAG

Prior to the Civil War, American flag makers had to import their fabric, called bunting, from Great Britain. In March 1865, General Benjamin F. Butler incorporated the United States Bunting Company in Lowell, Massachusetts, and began producing flag bunting in his factory. He exploited his ties with members of Congress and military officials to gain lucrative government contracts. By the mid 1880s, the factory employed 450 men and women, operated with five sets of cards, 5,000 spindles, and 220 looms. It used 3,000 pounds of wool per day. In 1866 an agent of the company, De Witt C. Farrington, presented the Senate with a large American flag measuring 12 by 21 feet to fly over the U.S. Capitol. It was reportedly the first flag of American-manufactured bunting to be hoisted over the Capitol building.

THE ORIGINS OF BUNTING

Bunting (or bunt) was originally a specific type of lightweight worsted wool fabric generically known as tammy, manufactured from the turn of the 17th century, and used for making ribbons and flags, including signal flags for the Royal Navy. The officer responsible for raising signals using flags is known as "bunts," a term still used for a ship's communications officer. Amongst other properties that made the fabric suitable for such uses was its high glaze, achieved by a process including hot-pressing.

ABOVE *Crowds gathered alongside decorated buildings for William McKinley's inaugural parade on March 4, 1897.*

ABOVE LEFT *The Southern Railway building dressed for Thomas Woodrow Wilson's inauguration on March 5, 1917.*

RIGHT *The U.S. Clothing Department building, dressed in 1865 to celebrate the end of the Civil War.*

OPPOSITE PAGE *The interior of the Old Post Office Pavilion is draped with flag bunting for a special occasion. The building then had its glass-covered atrium ceiling located on the ground floor.*

The Washington Post Building RAZED 1954

Built beginning in January of 1893, the Washington Post building at 1337 E Street, NW was meant to be a bold statement in a city teaming with competing daily newspapers. It was built at a cost of $55,000 to the designs of architect Appleton P. Clark, Jr. The owner of the *Post*, Beriah Wilkins, was apparently so pleased with the result that he hired Clark to design his own mansion at 1711 Massachusetts Avenue just nine years later (see Wilkins Mansion, page 85).

The *Post* was established by New Hampshire native Stilson Hutchins who printed the first edition on December 6, 1877. He had moved to Washington from Saint Louis, Missouri, where he served in the State legislature and had published several pro-Southern newspapers during the Civil War. Having absorbed the *Union*, the morning *National Republican* and the afternoon *Critic*, Hutchins was earning a salary of $32,000 at a time when the average city townhouse cost just $2,500 to build.

It wasn't the *Post* that made Hutchins a millionaire, however, but his financial backing of the linotype machine that transformed the printing industry. Invented by Ottmar Mergenthaler, it automated the assembly of tiny individual letters of raised lead that had to be hand assembled prior to the new machine. Hutchins sold the *Post* to focus on his new business in 1889.

New owner Beriah Wilkins bought out his partner Frank Hatton in 1889. As editor, he advocated for the government to change the practice of appointing new employees, and went on the attack of Theodore Roosevelt. He built the new office building of Indiana limestone at 1337 E Street, near the famed newspaper row on 14th Street.

John R. McLean, a publisher from Cincinnati, Ohio, purchased the *Post* in 1905. The paper focused on sensationalism to sell copies, and rapidly declined. McLean's son Edward B. McLean took over after his father's death in 1916, but by 1933 it was bankrupt.

The building and the *Post* were sold at auction on June 1, 1933 for $825,000 at the height of the Great Depression. The new buyer was Eugene Meyer, who had fortunately made a fortune on Wall Street before the stock market crash. He had also invested wisely during World War I in the Allied Chemical and Dye Corporation.

Meyer had the several hundreds of thousands of dollars necessary to improve the newspaper. He doubled circulation to 100,000 in just five years. But after he was appointed President of the new World Bank organization by President Harry Truman in 1946, he turned over control of the *Post* to his son-in-law, Philip L. Graham. A new building was built at 1513 L Street, NW in 1950, and just four years later, the *Post* became the city's largest newspaper when it purchased the *Washington Times-Herald*. The Washington Post building at 1337 E Street was razed in 1954.

Philip Graham created his own headline in 1963 when he committed suicide while under psychiatric care. In an unusual move for the era, his widow Katherine Graham assumed control of the paper. The world became aware of the newspaper's vast influence during the investigation of the Watergate affair from 1973 to 1974 by reporters Carl Bernstein and Bob Woodward. The scandal eventually led to the resignation of President Richard Nixon on August 9, 1974. Upon Katherine Graham's death in 2001, the *Post* was left to her son, Donald Graham.

OPPOSITE PAGE *The Washington Post building at 1337 E Street at the intersection with Pennsylvania Avenue. This circa-1910 photograph is looking north west, with the large Willard Hotel and columned Treasury Building in the distance.*

BELOW LEFT *Crowds gathered on the front steps of the building on June 1, 1933 to bid at auction for both the newspaper and its building.*

BELOW *The Washington Post Building in 1905, before construction of the east wing.*

Southwest Neighborhood RAZED 1960s

The Southwest quadrant has the distinction of being one of the oldest settled neighborhoods in the city. The city's smallest quadrant appears on the surface to be entirely built in the 1960s, but upon closer inspection, examples of architecture from the 1700s can be found amongst the Modernist high-rise apartment blocks.

Southwest D.C. is one of the most traumatic histories of neighborhoods in America that were subjected to 1950s idealistic planning concepts that called for the systematic razing of all buildings. The rich and diverse community that once existed there was viewed as urban decay, and virtually clear cut like a forest; tens of thousands of homes, businesses, churches, wharves, and warehouses were removed. Urban planning went from concept to reality between 1955 and 1965 as thousands of residents were displaced, most of whom would not have been able to return to a home that may have been owned by their family for five generations.

Populated by Native Americans and mapped by Captain John Smith in 1608, the area known as Southwest today was worked by enslaved persons in Maryland long before it became part of Pierre Charles L'Enfant's 1791 plan for the city. Land speculators built houses with varying degrees of success, a few of which remain, such as the circa-1794 Wheat Row.

Following the Civil War, Southwest had established itself as a vibrant community that boomed with thousands of row houses where freed blacks, and later Jewish and German immigrants lived. It would become the most diverse neighborhood in the city until its demise in the 1950s.

Southwest's existence as a neighborhood alive with children playing in the streets, baseball games in the local fields, and generations of families raising their children and teaching their business to the next of kin is no more. A series of events prompted the systematic demolition beginning in the mid 1950s. Images of the area had been used by Russian leaders as an example of the failure of Capitalism, and Congress was intent on erasing the blighted and crowded community that featured the U.S. Capitol in the background.

Efforts had been made as early as 1910 to publicize the city's crowded alleys with new buildings built by Washington Sanitary Housing Company. By the time a famous Supreme Court ruling of 1954 upheld the D.C. Redevelopment Act, passed in 1945 allowing imminent domain, much of the neighborhood had been vacated in anticipation of redevelopment.

The neighborhood was replaced with what was seen as innovative at the time, a mix of high-rise apartment and cooperative towers built alongside low-rise town homes, initially aimed at attracting a diverse ownership. By 1965, the whole community was reborn into a model neighborhood, with successes and failures in each project. Like the Oscar Niemeyer-designed Brazilian capital Brazilia, the Southwest neighborhood's reconstruction annhiliated most traces of its past.

Today, more than 60 years later, the community once again is gaining a history as its replacement buildings, construction methods, and its architects are being studied for their role in history. Apartment buildings themselves becoming desirable by fans of their architects. Little building in the last 50 years has infiltrated Southwest, and only with the introduction of new homes along the Southwest freeway in 2001 was a large-scale project undertaken in the community for the first time in nearly five decades.

LEFT *Crowded alley conditions were used to justify the need for their wholesale demolition as early as the 1950s.*

RIGHT *Images of deteriorated Southwest houses and alleys with the Capitol Building in the background were used by Russian leaders to illustrate the failure of capitalism.*

Horse Water Troughs REMOVED 1960

The horse population reached its peak in Washington, D.C. about 1904, and the brutally hot and humid summers often took its toll on the exhausted equines. About a decade earlier, in 1895, the D.C. Health Officer reported that a total of 4,846 dead animals (roughly 20 a day) had been brought to the Brown Garbage Crematory at the foot of South Capitol Street. Working conditions often took their toll on these horses, who were summarily dumped along the city's streets.

The Washington Humane Society set out to provide relief for the city's horses, and initiated a donation program to place more than 50 horse troughs throughout the city. Concerned residents could sponsor the cost of a trough, and have their name embossed on the metal.

Following the switch from horse to engine power, all troughs were removed by 1960. Several troughs made their way into front yards as planters. One trough was found discarded in Rock Creek Park, and another was donated to the Smithsonian's National Museum of American History. Several are also known to exist at the Bryant Street Pumping Station, while the fate of others remains unknown.

Although there might not be horses plying the streets of Washington anymore, if you look closely, there are remnants of their past existence. On 10th Street between O and P Streets, NW for example, one will find a wrought iron rein ring embedded into the granite curbstone, used for quickly securing a horse.

Further down 10th Street, between L and M Street, you'll find a stone step at the curb that was once used for mounting a horse or entering a carriage. Venture into an alley anywhere in the city, and you're likely to spot similar rings embedded into exterior brick walls to secure a horse while the carriage house or stall was being cleaned.

HORSING AROUND AT THE *POST*

Hugh Miller is seen below horsing around with a trough in 1924, when he was a staff photographer at *The Washington Post*. He photographed every presidential inaugural from Warren Harding's in 1921 to Lyndon B. Johnson's in 1963—except the first Franklin D. Roosevelt inaugural when Miller was a turf photographer for the *New York Morning Telegraph*. He went on to become one of the foremost turf photographers in the country. In the late 1940s, he concentrated on designing a state-of-the-art photographic laboratory for the new Washington Post building on L Street NW. When the roof of the Knickerbocker Theater collapsed in 1922, killing 98 people, Miller was the only photographer to get inside and snap pictures. He did that by pretending to be a welder. Among the many major disasters he covered during the period were a People's Drug warehouse fire, the Kann's warehouse fire, a tornado in La Plata, Maryland, and an explosion at the National Bureau of Standards laboratory (see page 115).

ABOVE *Pet ducklings are treated to a swim in the Dupont Circle horse trough.*

LEFT *Children enjoy a cool dunk from a hand-operated water spigot on the city streets.*

RIGHT *Hugh Miller, staff photographer on the* Post.

OPPOSITE PAGE *A "Horse Christmas Party" held in 1923 outside Washington's Humane Society offered free dinner and drinks for these young children bringing their horses to the event.*

Car Dealerships and Auto Showrooms

MOVED 1960

The first "horseless" vehicle arrived in Washington, D.C., to much fanfare in April of 1897, and during the next three decades, both the streetscape and several major commercial corridors such as 14th Street would change rapidly into automobile-centric business strips. The transformation got off to a slow start, however, as the early gasoline "buggies" often broke down and required hours of tinkering to ensure their mobility. Bystanders to these impromptu street repairs would often call out "get a horse," as many were unsure how the vehicles would ever transform into reliable transportation.

By 1929, however, there were over 135,000 automobiles registered to Washington residents, a fraction of what is registered on the street today (utilizing the same amount of space), but an impressive growth nonetheless. Just 30 years prior, a journey from Washington to Baltimore was something to talk about for weeks, and was frequently mentioned in the local newspapers. Travel was difficult, as early models either had to find fresh water for their boilers or a place to recharge batteries every 20 miles or so. The early use of batteries was soon discarded in favor of new and improved gasoline engines.

Automobile manufactures were aplenty in 1898, with hundreds competing in a new market for customers, including Washington's own Amzi Barber. (See Belmont Castle, page 44.) In March of 1898, Rudolph Jose opened the first automobile dealership in Washington at 1614 14th Street, NW to distribute the Kensington electric, manufactured in Buffalo, New York. That set the stage for buildings to be converted and new ones built along 14th Street corridor from Logan Circle to U Street and beyond.

Incredibly, by 1901, the auto business in the city was so great that Washington's first automobile show was held at the old Convention Hall to highlight the dozen or so models available for local purchase that year. The sale of automobiles also spurned the need for myriad parts and supplies companies that quickly filled in the smaller shops and former houses between the showrooms that lined 14th Street. The influx of cars and new drivers also created a multitude of crashes and confusion at the city's many intersections, where the previous accustomed speed was that of a trotting horse.

The Standard Automotive Supply Company was located in the ground floor of the Hudson apartment building on the northwest corner of 14th and S Streets. Next door (at 1802 14th Street), the French mansard styled building built in the 1870s housed a new and used tire store.

As commercial trends evolved and automobile companies moved out of the city to large lots in the suburbs, the former showrooms were converted into everything from apartments to churches.

OPPOSITE PAGE *A circa-1915 photograph of the Trew Motor Company showroom on 14th Street.*

BOTTOM *A Christmas 1922 window display at the Oldsmobile Sales Company on Connecticut Avenue.*

ABOVE *The well-stocked Standard Automotive Supply Company store on the ground floor of the Hudson apartment building.*

Washington Streetcars DISMANTLED 1962

For nearly 100 years, between 1862 and 1962, streetcars in Washington, D.C. transported residents throughout the city and into the emerging suburbs like Chevy Chase, Maryland, built especially with streetcars in mind.

The first streetcars in the city were drawn by horses and carried people short distances on flat terrain. With the introduction of cleaner and faster electric streetcars, capable of climbing steep inclines, the city found itself able easily to expand into the hilly suburbs north of the old city and in Anacostia. There were a multitude of companies operating and competing for paid passenger travel. Several of the District's streetcar lines were extended into Maryland, and two Virginia lines crossed into the District.

For a brief time, the city experimented with cable cars, but by the beginning of the 20th century, the streetcar system had been fully electrified. Later the extensive mergers of the competing operators was dubbed the "Great Streetcar Consolidation"

resulted in most of the local transit firms being merged into two major companies, and in 1933, all streetcars were brought under one company, Capital Transit.

The streetcars in turn began to face competition from the automobile, and buses. Some projects were implemented to separate automobile cars and streetcars, like the Dupont Underground station, completed under Dupont Circle in 1949. Streetcars descended down a ramp to a subterranean station stop, and re-emerged on the other side of the circle to join traffic, running down the center of Connecticut Avenue.

After a labor strike in 1955 that lasted seven weeks, the company changed ownership and became D.C. Transit. It operated 750 buses and 450 streetcars, but the sale mandated that the company phase out all remaining streetcars. The system was dismantled in the early 1960s and the last streetcar ran on January 28, 1962.

OPPOSITE PAGE *A streetcar on Pennsylvania Avenue near Eighth Street, NW.*

BELOW LEFT *A streetcar rounds the corner at B Street and Delaware Avenue in 1910.*

BELOW *A touring car with a precarious staircase and second story open seating takes visitors along the Eckington and Soldiers Home line.*

BOTTOM *Passengers loading a crowded streetcar at 11th and F Streets, NW about 1920.*

Rochambeau Apartment Building **RAZED 1962**

The fabled Rochambeau Apartment building was built overlooking Farragut Square at 815 Connecticut Avenue by Francis Henry Duehay beginning in June of 1903. Its luxury apartments housed many of the Washington elite, including Congressmen and a Supreme Court Justice, for the next 30 years, until it was rented as an office building.

Duehay received his building permit on June 19, 1903, and estimated that the cost of construction would be $500,000. It was designed by noted local prolific architect and developer, Thomas Franklin Schneider.

During the winter of 1905, owner Duehay was arrested for allegedly violating the new anti-smoke law in Washington, which was enacted to reduce the amount of thick black smoke emanating from factories and businesses. It exempted private residences, of course, and Duehay argued in an eventual lawsuit that the apartment house was indeed a private residence and not a commercial building.

Duehay had been born in Washington, D.C., in 1863, and graduated from the National Law School. Almost immediately after leaving school, he established the F. H. Duehay real estate company that specialized in apartment buildings. He and his wife Edith resided for most of their lives at 1623 28th Street, NW. Incidentally, he served as the superintendent of federal prisons during World War I.

The Rochambeau was sold to the Acacia Mutual Life Insurance Company for $650,000 in early 1935. On November 1, 1935, the federal government took over the apartment house, and notified its 100 residents, mostly doctors and dentists, to vacate their apartments by December 1st of that year, so the building could be converted in offices for the

Federal Trade Commission. At the time, Supreme Court Associate Justice James Clark McReynolds was among its more prominent occupants. President Franklin Roosevelt's New Deal prompted the establishments of thousands of new federal workers, and office space in Washington quickly became scarce.

Duehay died of a heart attack in 1934 at the age of 70 and was interred in Oak Hill cemetery in Georgetown. His Rochambeau apartment building was torn down in 1962 for a modern office building.

ABOVE The Rochambeau Apartment seen from across Farragut Square, with the Army & Navy Club located next door.

FAR LEFT Architect Thomas Franklin Schneider.

LEFT Supreme Court Associate Justice James Clark McReynolds, a resident of the Rochambeau.

RIGHT The highly ornamented facade of the Rochambeau Apartment building at 815 Connecticut Avenue, NW.

Providence Hospital REMODELED 1904, RAZED 1964

Of the nine city hospitals in Washington during the 19th century, the Second Empire-styled building at Second and D Streets, SE had been completed in 1872 after six years of construction. It featured 27 apartment rooms for patients in the central portion, with each wing divided into five large wards. It held a total of 250 beds.

The hospital itself had been formed when the city's only civilian hospital, the Washington Infirmary on Judiciary Square, was seized by Union army officials on the eve of the Civil War for the exclusive use of treating injured soldiers. Washington doctors, led by Dr. Joseph M. Toner, approached the Sisters of Charity in Maryland to assemble a team of nuns to come to the city and assist in forming a new civilian hospital.

Fortunately, a large wood frame house at Second and D Streets, SE was available for rent by the widow of Marine Corps Major Augustus Nicholson, and the first patient was admitted on June 27, 1861. During the war, the remainder of the vacant block was soon filled with army tents, and the doctors treated those that flooded into Washington with various wounds from the conflict, civilians and military alike.

Meanwhile, the Sisters had begun to purchase all the remaining lots on the Square, and successfully lobbied Congress for financial awards in 1866 and again in 1868, due to their commitment to treating soldiers during the war. These grants led to the construction of the brick building which began in 1866.

Under the guidance of Sister Beatrice Duffy from 1869 to 1899, Providence Hospital bloomed into a first-class institution that would develop a number of innovative techniques and procedures. A new surgical amphitheater was built in 1882 to train doctors and nurses who watched live surgeries in the round seating. Elaborate private suites could be rented by the wealthy.

The Sisters provided the first social work for the city's poor, feeding them from a soup kitchen in the basement, and teaching mothers how to shop economically and for proper nutrition. In 1896, a nursing school opened, the first three-year degree program in the country. The new technology of X-rays was installed that same year. In 1899, a separate infectious ward was established to prevent disease from spreading from patient to patient.

The building was completely remodeled by architect Waddy B. Wood into a Spanish Revival-style in 1904, which altered the look of the building forever. He added a 175-foot tall watch tower at the center so that patients could gain a rare look over the city.

Like many buildings that need to change when new technology is introduced, by 1947 Providence Hospital was showing its age and was becoming overcrowded. A new complex was built at 12th and Varnum Streets, NW, which opened in 1956. The old building was purchased by the federal government to house employees of the Commerce Department, and was eventually abandoned in 1964 when it was razed for a parking lot.

OPPOSITE PAGE *The massive Providence Hospital at Second and D Streets, SE.*

BELOW *The staff of Providence Hospital photographed in about 1895.*

Watergate Floating Theater DISMANTLED 1965

The large steps located behind the Lincoln Memorial were originally intended to receive visitors and dignitaries arriving in style aboard water taxis, but they never served that function. Instead, they were the perfect place from which to watch a stage production or theatrical performance on an anchored barge known affectionately as the Watergate Theater. Rented from the Navy, its popular summer productions began in 1935.

The first production was a concert by the National Symphony Orchestra, under the direction of Hans Kindler, on July 14, 1935. The program closed with Tchaikovsky's "1812 Overture".

The concerts became known as "Sunset Symphonies," and they were extremely popular. The National Park Service estimated that by 1946, two million people had attended performances. In 1948, a much larger and elaborate barge was built at a cost of $75,000.

The theater eventually attracted Hollywood names such as Frank Sinatra and Paul Robeson.

FLOATING AROUND A NEW THEATER IDEA

As strange as it sounds, the Watergate Floating Theater was not that unusual in its conception. For almost 30 years, the Adams Floating Theater drifted into towns all over the Chesapeake Bay between 1914 and 1941, from its home port of Leonardstown, Maryland. It even made it all the way to North Carolina. It was a large houseboat pushed by tugboats that housed actors and actresses, cooks, and management onboard for the summer. It brought plays and dramas to small and large cities alike. Writer Edna Ferber spent several days with the theater in North Carolina as a basis for her wildly popular novel and later musical, "Show Boat", which she set in Mississippi. And the trend may continue: Spike Parrish and other floating theater enthusiasts have recently created the Chesapeake Floating Theatre in the Indian Head Center for the Arts and are producing a limited number of plays under the name Black Box Theater.

Another Watergate performer was the soprano Lillian Evans Tibbs (1890–1967), professionally known as Madame Lillian Evanti. She was the first black woman to sing opera with an organized company in Europe.

The concerts ceased in 1962 when the jet service began at Washington National Airport, making too much noise for programs to continue. Paul Hume wrote a headline in *The Washington Post* that read "The Jets Played the Finale." The Watergate Theater lent its name to the infamous Watergate apartment complex which was built on the Potomac to the north beginning in 1967.

ABOVE LEFT *African American opera singer Madame Lillian Evanti (1890–1967).*

LEFT *Instead of standing up in a canoe for the playing of the National Anthem, crowds raised their paddles.*

RIGHT *Thousands of residents and tourists watched summer productions at the Watergate Floating Theater.*

Griffith Stadium RAZED 1965

The young Washingtonians attending a baseball game at the new National Park may not know that Washington once had a major stadium that stood for over 50 years. It was located between the residential neighborhoods of Le Droit Park, Greater U Street, and Shaw. Businessman and former Chicago White Stockings hero Clark Griffith built the large stadium near the intersection of Seventh and V Streets, NW. At the time, the area was one of the oldest established residential communities in the city, and the stadium literally abutted the surrounding two-story townhouses. Its towering lights could be seen for 15 blocks.

The site of Griffith Stadium was first a large open park on which the National League baseball team played beginning in 1886. Starting in 1905, it was utilized by the Washington American League team before Clark Griffith built the partly covered stadium in 1914; it was named after him in 1924. Before Griffith moved to Washington to take over the team, it was apparently expected for the city's baseball team to land in last place, with the standing joke around the country being "Washington, First in War, First in Peace, but Last in the American League."

Despite that mockery, as early as 1868, 4,000 Washington baseball fans were gathering for Saturday games on the White House lawn. In 1870, local baseball rule expert Mike Scanlon built the first baseball park in the city at 17th and S Street, with 500 seats and an admission price of just 25 cents!

The Washington Senators baseball team called Griffith Stadium home, and went on to beat the New York Giants there to capture the World Series title in 1924. It was the first series to be opened and attended by a U.S. President. Griffith was also used by African American teams including the Washington Elite Giants, the Le Droit Tigers, the Washington Pilots, and the Homestead Grays. Josh Gibson, considered by many to be the best Negro League player of all time, won nine home run titles in his 13 seasons for the Homestead Grays.

As a neighborhood institution, Griffith Stadium was a celebrated arena, host to all cultures and a variety of events. It was one of the very few public places in Washington that was never segregated, although most of its teams were. Fans at Griffith may have attended major league or Howard University baseball, National Negro League

A MONUMENTAL CATCH

The desire to prove baseball-playing superiority by actually catching a ball thrown from the top of the Washington Monument had begun to be attempted in 1894. It took 14 years of practice, but the feat was finally accomplished on August 21, 1908 by Gabby Street, during his 13th attempt. The catch was taken with such force that it knocked Street to the ground, although he was able to retain the ball in his mitt to the delight of the watching crowd.

baseball, religious revivals, Howard University football, high school drill competitions, or even the first games of the Redskins, who played here from 1937, until they moved to RFK Stadium in 1961. Local schools also used the arena for sports and recreation activities.

Clark Griffith died in 1955, and his son Calvin moved the Senators to Minneapolis in 1960. Five years later, the stadium was razed to accommodate the expansion of the Howard University Hospital.

LEFT *Assistant Secretary of the Navy Franklin D. Roosevelt (third from right) walks the Washington Senators onto the field at Griffith Stadium on the opening day of baseball, 1917.*

RIGHT *This aerial view of Griffith Stadium taken on July 1, 1937, shows just how close it was located to the surrounding townhouses.*